College English **3**

Advanced

KMU CE3 Committee

Keimyung University Press

Contents

UNIT **1-1**

Caring about What Others Think

Scan and find the tracks.

READING 1

SKILLS

Reading Skill:
Making Connections

Critical-Thinking Skill:
Detecting Arguments

WARM-UP QUESTIONS

1. What kinds of situations might make people feel awkward or embarrassed?
2. How would you like people to think of you—as clever, beautiful, caring, etc.? Why?
3. Can you think of any situations where caring about what others think might be helpful? Detrimental?
4. How do you feel about the idea of having different "faces" for different people or situations?
5. Have you ever come across the advice to "be yourself"? What are your initial thoughts on this advice?

BEFORE YOU READ

Read the statements. Check (✓) whether you agree or disagree with each statement. Discuss your answers with a partner.

	Strongly disagree	Disagree somewhat	Agree somewhat	Strongly agree
1. I always do my best to appear good in public.				
2. I like to follow trends that my friends are following.				
3. I do everything I can to avoid embarrassment.				
4. I talk to different people in different ways.				
5. I care less now about what people think of me than I used to.				

VOCABULARY PREVIEW

1 Read the sentences. Circle the words closest in meaning to the words in bold.

1. Did the writer think about what would happen if everyone **ceased** to care about what others think?
   a. stopped　b. attempted　c. imagined

2. Many **psychologists** believe that humans developed emotions in order to survive.
   a. patients　b. scientists　c. surgeons

3. If we **deviate** from social conventions too often, we might end up unpopular and alone.
   a. discuss　b. lie　c. differ

4. You make an embarrassing mistake; **subsequently**, you try to avoid repeating it.
   a. luckily　b. later　c. seemingly

5. If we don't care about what others think of us, we don't **adapt** our personalities and grow.
   a. alter　b. keep　c. trust

6. We present a certain **image** of ourselves around others that shows we care about their expectations.
   a. argument　b. value　c. idea

7. The way we talk and behave **functions** to show others that we care about their opinion.
   a. allows　b. drives　c. works

8. As **intelligent** creatures, we care about what others think of us.
   a. smart　b. friendly　c. emotional

2 Match the words in bold in section 1 above to their definitions below.

________ : to change something so that it functions better or is better suited for a purpose

________ : to bring an activity or action to an end

________ : to stray, especially from a standard, principle, or topic

________ : to work; to operate

________ : the idea that people have about someone or something

________ : able to learn and understand things

________ : a person who specializes in the study of mind and behavior or in the treatment of mental, emotional, and behavioral disorders

________ : at a later time

CARING ABOUT WHAT OTHERS THINK

Track 01

1. **Reading Skill: Making Connections**
   You can better understand a reading if you connect it with things you already know. A text-to-text connection relates the passage to another text. A text-to-self connection relates the passage to yourself. A text-to-world connection relates the passage to your knowledge.

2. **Critical-Thinking Skill: Detecting Arguments**
   An argument is an attempt to prove that something is true. To find an argument, you must identify the premises and the conclusion that follows.

Today, many self-help books claim to have the recipe for healthy, wealthy, and wise living; one of their most frequent suggestions is "be yourself." As Roy T. Bennett's *The Light in the Heart* advises, readers should "stop caring about what others think." As with many **clichés**[1], there may be some wisdom behind Bennett's advice. Certainly, worrying too much about others' opinions can be stressful and leave us feeling doubtful and depressed, but have writers like Bennett considered the effects of everyone on earth ceasing to care about how they are perceived?

Emotions such as embarrassment and **shame**[2] are usually the result of feeling as though we've made a mistake in the eyes of others—they don't feel good, but they serve an important purpose. Imagine you are walking to the supermarket check-out. You are not paying attention and accidentally cut in front of someone in line. Another customer points out your mistake, and you head to the back of the line. How do you feel? Slightly embarrassed, maybe? This is because you have broken a social convention: these are the small, everyday codes and rules that we live by, and they are essential to the smooth running of societies.

Embarrassment and shame prove that humans **instinctively**[3] care about what people think of them. But why should this be? Cutting in line would be helpful for us, right? Well, while emotions

1 **cliché** *n.* a saying or remark that is often made and is therefore not original or interesting
2 **shame** *n.* an uncomfortable feeling of guilt caused by someone's bad behavior
3 **instinctively** *adv.* in a way that is not thought about, planned, or developed by training

such as embarrassment help maintain a healthy society, many psychologists argue that humans actually developed them for **self-preservation**[4]. Suppose we deviate from social conventions too often. In that case, we may soon find ourselves alone, without friends, and on the margins of our society—something we instinctively know would not benefit us as individuals.

Also, without these painfully memorable emotions, we are likely to repeat our mistakes. We can illustrate the personal learning value of embarrassment more clearly with another example. Let's imagine you've now left the supermarket. You didn't remember to bring a bag, so you are struggling to hold many loose apples, oranges, and bananas. Suddenly, you lose your grip, your precious fruit rolls all over the busy street, and you are left desperately chasing after it. If you are feeling embarrassed again, as might be expected, then subsequently, you'll probably remember to bring a shopping bag to get your food home safely.

"Not caring about what others think" suggests that whatever the situation, we should not change or adapt our personalities—instead, as the saying goes, we should "be true to ourselves." In English, the idea of being "two-faced" is extremely negative and is used to describe people who are **deceptive**[5] or false. Of course, most of us know it's usually not healthy—or even helpful—to lie or **consciously**[6] pretend to be someone else. However, is it such a bad thing to have more than one "face"? For example, most of us would naturally find ourselves talking very differently to our ten-year-old niece, eighty-year-old grandmother, boss, and best friend. The image we present around others functions as a sign that we are thinking about their expectations, and the adaptations we make are signs of empathy—they show that we have considered others' thoughts, needs, and feelings.

In fact, there is a saying that we have *three* distinct faces: one for the world, one for our families, and one for ourselves. This seems quite realistic; however, it might also suggest that the last of these faces is the true or "real" one. Can we really say that we are most honestly ourselves when we are alone? Most psychologists argue that we are just as capable of lying to ourselves as we are to others, so perhaps it's other people's opinions of us that "keep us honest."

As with many things in life, the truth probably lies somewhere in between. Worrying too much about how we are seen could be a waste of time—or even dangerous, especially if it is based on shallow **judgments**[7] about what we wear or how we look. On the other hand, being concerned about how others view us as intelligent, emotional creatures is essential to our well-being and the success of our communities.

4	**self-preservation**	*n.*	behavior based on feelings that warn people to protect themselves
5	**deceptive**	*adj.*	making someone believe something that is not true
6	**consciously**	*adv.*	in a way that is determined and intentional
7	**judgment**	*n.*	a decision or opinion about someone or something

COMPREHENSION CHECK-UPS

1. According to paragraph 1, all of the following are true of self-help books EXCEPT ________.

a. they advise readers not to worry about others' opinions
b. they claim they can make you rich, well, and wise
c. they can make us feel unsure and lead to sadness
d. they often repeat ideas that are not original or helpful

2. According to paragraph 2, why might shame be useful to society?

a. Because it stops people from trying to do dangerous things
b. Because the economy relies on us doing as we are told
c. Because supermarkets are busy and need order to operate
d. Because everyone benefits when people maintain the rules

3. Read paragraph 2 and write an example of breaking a social convention.

____

____

4. In paragraph 2, why does the author ask, "How do you feel?"

a. To make the reader imagine someone offending them
b. To question what people become embarrassed about
c. To force the reader to imagine breaking an unofficial rule
d. To show the reader that they care about their feelings

5. According to paragraph 4, why might embarrassment be useful to individuals?

a. Because it lets other people know that they care
b. Because it helps us remember mistakes we have made
c. Because we would treat each other badly without it
d. Because it stops us from being too arrogant

6. According to paragraph 5, which of the following is NOT true?

a. We communicate with different people in different ways.
b. People think that behaving differently around others is dishonest.
c. Being described as "two-faced" is a compliment.
d. When we change our behavior, it shows we care about others.

7. What can be inferred from paragraph 5?

   a. People who don't change their behavior are dishonest.
   b. People who expect others to change are unreasonable.
   c. People who treat others differently are not successful.
   d. People who always act the same way lack empathy.

8. Read paragraph 5. Describe how you talk to people differently. Use specific examples.

   ____

   ____

9. According to paragraph 6, what is the problem with the saying?

   a. It implies we are only ourselves when no one else is there.
   b. It assumes that people everywhere are the same.
   c. It suggests each of us is three different people.
   d. It is not relevant because it comes from a different time.

10. Which statement best restates the sentence, "Worrying too much about how we are seen could be a waste of time—or even dangerous, especially if it is based on shallow judgments about what we wear or how we look." from paragraph 7?

   a. Worrying about the clothes we wear is natural because we need them.
   b. Caring about what people think is unavoidable, so we need to accept it.
   c. Being concerned about what people think is something we grow out of.
   d. Stressing over one's appearance can be a waste of time and even harmful.

MAPPING IDEAS

Read the sentences about the passage. Which phrases best complete the sentences according to the given types of connections? Circle the correct letters.

1. **Text-to-text:** The mention of worrying about other people's opinions too much made me think about . . .

   a. an article I read about online bullying and how it can affect young people.
   b. a friend who is always stressed about their appearance.

2. **Text-to-self:** The example of the shopping bag made me think of . . .

   a. how difficult it must be to work at a grocery store.
   b. the time when I tripped and fell while looking at my phone.

3. **Text-to-self:** The topic of having more than one face made me think of . . .
   a. how it is difficult for many people to make good friends.
   b. the last time I saw my grandparents and how I talked to them.

4. **Text-to-world:** The mention of shallow judgments made me think of . . .
   a. how people place value on designer labels and the latest trends.
   b. an article on the latest changes in the fashion industry.

Now make your own connections.

1. **Text-to-text:** The mention of worrying about other people's opinions too much made me think about . . .

   ____

2. **Text-to-self:** The example of the shopping bag made me think of . . .

   ____

3. **Text-to-world:** The mention of shallow judgments made me think of . . .

   ____

VOCABULARY REVIEW

Fill in the blanks with the correct words from the box. Change the form if needed.

cease	psychologist	deviate	adapt
function	intelligent	shame	judgment

1. Jake wants to be a(n) ______________ because he is interested in the human mind.
2. Those who ______________ seriously from rules and laws may find themselves in prison.
3. We should try and get to know people before passing ______________ on them.
4. The factory will ______________ operations this Friday for a national holiday.
5. Road signs ______________ as a way to keep traffic under control.
6. You shouldn't feel ______________ when you fail at something despite trying your best.
7. Kyle is extremely ______________, so other students often ask him for help.
8. When children change schools, it can sometimes be difficult for them to ______________.

CRITICAL-THINKING SKILL

Detecting Arguments

An argument is an attempt to prove that something is true. Simple arguments use one or more statements (called premises) to build a conclusion. For example:

(1) Research shows that people who exercise daily have a lower risk of heart disease.

(2) I want to reduce my risk of heart disease.

(3) Therefore, I should exercise daily.

1 Read the excerpt. Evaluate it with a partner and complete the activities.

Imagine you are walking to the supermarket check-out. You are not paying attention and accidentally cut in front of someone in line. Another customer points out your mistake, and you head to the back of the line. How do you feel? Slightly embarrassed, maybe? This is because you have broken a social convention: these are the small, everyday codes and rules that we live by, and they are essential to the smooth running of societies.

DETECTING ARGUMENTS Based on the information in the excerpt, circle the most logical conclusion that could be drawn.

a. Caring about what others think is important because it makes us unique.

b. Humans are selfish and don't care what others think, but they want to seem honest.

c. Embarrassment is necessary to ensure that people follow social conventions.

d. Rules like going to the back of the line exist to make us feel embarrassed.

2 Write a short summary that includes two or three premises that support the conclusion you circled.

IDEAS IN DISCUSSION

1. The article argues for a middle ground between not caring at all and obsessing over what others think. How can we find this balance in our daily lives? What are some signs that we might be caring too much or too little about other people's opinions?

2. The article suggests that embarrassment and shame serve a purpose in society. Do you agree? Can you think of other emotions that might serve a similar function? Are there situations where these emotions might be unhelpful? How can we learn from them constructively?

3. The article challenges the idea of being completely true to ourselves at all times. Is it ever okay to adapt our behavior depending on the situation? What are the potential benefits and drawbacks of having different "faces" for different people? When might this become inauthentic?

4. The article suggests that other people's opinions can actually help to "keep us honest." Do you agree? How can the way others perceive us influence who we become? Can we truly know ourselves without considering the perspectives of others?

5. Should self-help books focus more on finding balance rather than absolutes like "be yourself"? How does social media play a role in how much we care about what others think? Can cultural background influence how much we value the opinions of others?

IDEAS IN WRITING

1. **The Psychological Impact of Embarrassment and Shame:** Analyze the argument that humans have developed emotions like embarrassment for self-preservation and to avoid social exclusion. Explore how feelings of embarrassment and shame influence individual behavior and personal growth. Use real-life examples.

2. **The Duality of "Be Yourself" and Social Adaptation:** How can we care about others' opinions without letting them control us? Examine the tension between the self-help advice to "be yourself" and the need to adapt to social expectations and norms.

3. **The Role of Social Conventions in Maintaining Societal Order:** Explore how social conventions, such as queueing behavior, are essential for the smooth functioning of societies and how emotions like embarrassment and shame reinforce these conventions. Does caring about how we are perceived contribute to a functioning community? Why does our concern for others' opinions matter for society's well-being?

4. **The Concept of Multiple "Faces" in Social Interactions:** Evaluate the idea that people present different "faces" or personas in various social contexts and discuss the implications of this behavior for personal authenticity and social empathy. Explore strategies for balancing the desire to be true to oneself with the need to meet social expectations and norms.

5. **Cultural Context:** Analyze a specific historical event or social movement where caring about public opinion played a significant role. Explore the spectrum of identity in our interactions with others. Compare and contrast the concept of "caring about what others think" across different cultures. How can we navigate the delicate balance between respecting social norms and asserting our personal values in our cultural context?

ETHICS & PHILOSOPHY

UNIT 1-2 Plant-Powered Living

Scan and find the tracks.

READING 2

SKILLS

Reading Skill:
Identifying the Author's Point of View

Critical-Thinking Skill:
Considering Objections

WARM-UP QUESTIONS

1. How would you describe your diet?
2. What do you know about vegetarianism?
3. Do you consider the environment when choosing what to eat?
4. Is vegetarianism becoming more common in your country?
5. Are you or would you consider becoming vegetarian? Why or why not?

BEFORE YOU READ

Read the statements. Check (✓) whether you agree or disagree with each statement. Discuss your answers with a partner.

	Strongly disagree	Disagree somewhat	Agree somewhat	Strongly agree
1. Being a vegetarian is better for the environment.				
2. There's nothing wrong with eating meat.				
3. Vegetarians are healthier than non-vegetarians.				
4. Becoming a vegetarian is not easy.				
5. There are many issues in the food industry that need to be fixed.				

VOCABULARY PREVIEW

1 Read the sentences. Circle the words closest in meaning to the words in bold.

1. Vegetarians avoid food products **derived** from animals.
   a. made   b. served   c. defined

2. Vegetarianism is pretty **straightforward**, and there are a lot of benefits to it.
   a. hard   b. truthful   c. clear

3. Some vegetarian diets **exclude** certain food products from animals but include others.
   a. ban   b. accept   c. destroy

4. Studies **conducted** by a professional research company show that vegetarianism is on the rise in the US.
   a. challenged   b. performed   c. taught

5. Most vegetarians eat foods that are less **processed** and have fewer chemicals.
   a. treated   b. cleaned   c. natural

6. A vegetarian needs enough **diversity** in their diet to stay healthy.
   a. interest   b. thickness   c. variety

7. Vegetarians can take dietary **supplements** to stay healthy.
   a. medicines   b. extras   c. lessons

8. Vegetarian diets can provide the full **complement** of vitamins, minerals, and other things humans need to be healthy.
   a. achievement   b. measure   c. choice

2 Match the words in bold in section 1 above to their definitions below.

________ : a number of people or things that complete something or make it better

________ : to organize and perform a particular activity

________ : to get something from something else

________ : the quality or state of having many different forms, types, etc.

________ : to intentionally not include something

________ : (of food) having had some sort of chemical or industrial treatment in order to cook it, preserve it, or improve its taste or appearance

________ : easy to understand; simple

________ : something that is added to something else in order to make it complete

PLANT-POWERED LIVING

Track 02

1. **Reading Skill: Identifying the Author's Point of View**
   A point of view is the attitude or position a person takes on a subject. A neutral point of view doesn't choose sides. A biased point of view is either influenced by outside factors or the writer's opinion.

2. **Critical-Thinking Skill: Considering Objections**
   An important part of critical thinking is considering objections to the author's points. Objections are ideas, factors, or examples that suggest the author's points are incorrect.

The basic principle of vegetarianism is simple: eat plant-based food products and not food products derived from animals. Although this idea is pretty straightforward, the wonderful world of vegetarianism doesn't end there. To some people, this lifestyle seems strange. There are those who see vegetarians as having radical views or being **malnourished**[1]. But in reality, what it means to be a vegetarian is poorly understood. The actual reasons for becoming vegetarian are diverse, as are the kinds of plant-based diets. By learning a little more about vegetarianism, you can see why people choose this lifestyle and how it can help you live a longer, healthier, and more environmentally friendly life.

According to the Mayo Clinic's *In-Depth Nutrition and Healthy Eating* guide, there are six basic types of vegetarians. A lacto-vegetarian follows a diet that excludes food products containing meat, fish, **poultry**[2], and eggs but includes dairy products like milk, cheese, and yogurt. Next, ovo-vegetarians exclude meat, poultry, seafood, and dairy products but allow eggs. The third kind of vegetarian is a sort of mixture of the first two types. Lacto-ovo vegetarian diets exclude meat, fish, and poultry but allow both dairy products and eggs. Fourth are pescatarians, who exclude all animal-based foods except fish. Fifth is a vegan diet, which is the most limited. It excludes all foods that contain meat, poultry, fish, eggs, or dairy products. Sixth is the least

[1] **malnourished** *adj.* not having enough food or enough healthy food
[2] **poultry** *n.* birds kept for eggs or meat

limited—sometimes called a semi-vegetarian or a "flexitarian" diet. People who follow this diet mostly eat plants but include animal products in small amounts.

Now that we understand the various types of vegetarian diets, let's look at why people choose to become vegetarians. According to a study conducted by Ipsos Retail Performance, a market research firm, there has been a 300-percent increase in the number of vegetarians from 2004 to 2019 in the US. Nearly ten million Americans now consider themselves vegetarians. There are various reasons for making this choice, including religion, environmental impact, morals, and health. Perhaps the least clear and easily understood among these reasons is the environmental impact. Farm animals that provide food products require a lot of land to raise. And massive amounts of energy are required to provide them with shelter, food, and transportation. Also, farm animals, particularly cows, create methane—a greenhouse gas. In the US, it's estimated that agriculture is responsible for ten percent of all emissions.

After becoming vegetarian, many people notice both immediate and long-lasting improvements to their health. Most plant-based diets contain foods that are less processed and have fewer chemicals. Eating more natural and less processed food means you are more likely to have lower blood sugar, which reduces your risk of diabetes. Furthermore, one Harvard Medical School study shows that plant-based diets can lower your **cholesterol**[3], reduce the risk of many serious illnesses, and extend your life. Many fruits, vegetables, and seeds are loaded with **antioxidants**[4] that help the body fight diseases and repair damaged **tissue**[5].

While removing certain things from your diet has obvious benefits, people sometimes worry that a vegetarian diet can lead to poor **nutrition**[6]. One common misunderstanding about vegetarianism is the idea that a plant-based diet cannot provide sufficient nutrition. It's true that some things humans need are only or mostly found in animal products. No plant-based food by itself contains complete **proteins**[7], and only animal products can provide vitamin B12 and the kind of iron that our bodies absorb most easily. But research shows that with enough diversity, along with supplements, your body can have the full complement of **nutrients**[8] that it requires.

Becoming a vegetarian comes with a lot of choices. You can choose your reasons for doing so and choose the vegetarian diet that is best for you. As a bonus, the benefits extend beyond just you. Not only might you live a longer, healthier life, you will also help protect the environment.

[3] **cholesterol** *n.* a type of fat in your body that can cause heart disease if you have too much of it
[4] **antioxidant** *n.* a substance in the body that protects cells from damage caused by free radicals (unstable molecules)
[5] **tissue** *n.* the material that animals and plants are made of
[6] **nutrition** *n.* eating the right kinds of foods to promote growth and health
[7] **protein** *n.* a substance found in foods such as eggs, milk, and meat that is important to the human diet
[8] **nutrient** *n.* a substance that an animal needs to eat or a plant needs from the soil in order to live and grow

COMPREHENSION CHECK-UPS

1. All of the following are stated in paragraph 1 EXCEPT ________.

   a. the concept of vegetarianism is easy to understand
   b. some people think vegetarians have strange views
   c. people become vegetarian for many different reasons
   d. it is fairly common for vegetarians to be malnourished

2. According to paragraph 2, which type of vegetarian eats eggs and cheese but not fish?

   a. A lacto-vegetarian
   b. A lacto-ovo vegetarian
   c. A vegan
   d. A pescatarian

3. According to paragraph 3, what is one reason why some people choose to become vegetarians?

   a. Peer pressure
   b. Social trends
   c. Environmental impact
   d. Effective advertising

4. Read paragraph 3 and write why animal farming is bad for the environment.

   ____

   ____

5. Which of the following is true according to paragraph 4?

   a. Some benefits of becoming vegetarian happen quickly.
   b. Many vegetarians see an increase in blood sugar.
   c. A Harvard study found that cholesterol isn't harmful.
   d. Animal products do not contain antioxidants.

6. Which statement best restates the sentence, "Many fruits, vegetables, and seeds are loaded with antioxidants that help the body fight diseases and repair damaged tissue." from paragraph 4?

a. Fruits and other plant products contain antioxidants.
b. Certain plant-based foods are thought to cure disease and heal tissue.
c. Foods from plants help the body to manufacture antioxidants.
d. Plant-based foods contain substances that help keep the body healthy.

7. According to paragraph 5, which of the following is true?

a. Vegetarians consume more complete proteins than non-vegetarians.
b. Supplements can be useful to people on a vegetarian diet.
c. Vitamin B12 is found in a variety of plant-based foods.
d. Vegetarians can get all the nutrients they need from plants.

8. In paragraph 5, why does the author mention iron?

a. To give an example of a nutrient that vegetarians typically get more of
b. To give an example of a supplement that most vegetarians take
c. To give an example of a nutrient not found in vegetarian diets
d. To give an example of a supplement that is made from animal products

9. Read paragraph 6. What is the author's main purpose for writing this passage?

a. To sell something
b. To educate and persuade
c. To give information
d. To analyze a problem and offer solutions

10. What can be inferred about the author's opinion from paragraph 6?

a. That vegetarianism is good for some people but not others
b. That there is no single correct reason to be vegetarian
c. That everyone will eventually become vegetarian
d. That the best kind of vegetarian diet is a vegan diet

MAPPING IDEAS

Read the sentences and match them to the best points of view in the graphic organizer.

STATEMENTS

1. The basic principles of vegetarianism are simple: eat plant-based food products and do not eat food products derived from animals.
2. Although this idea is pretty straightforward, the wonderful world of vegetarianism doesn't end there.
3. But in reality, what it means to be a vegetarian is poorly understood.
4. According to the Mayo Clinic's *In-Depth Nutrition and Healthy Eating* guide, there are six basic types of vegetarians.
5. There are various reasons for making this choice, including religion, environmental impact, morals, and health.
6. Becoming a vegetarian comes with a lot of choices.

POINTS OF VIEW	
A. NEUTRAL	**B. BIASED**

VOCABULARY REVIEW

Fill in the blanks with the correct words from the box. Change the form if needed.

conduct	**exclude**	**processed**	**protein**
antioxidant	**supplement**	**straightforward**	**derived**

1. Green tea is well-known for having ______________, making it healthier than soda.
2. Meat, fish, and other animal products contain a lot of ______________.
3. This list of the best movies of the year isn't complete because it ______________ foreign films.
4. The study was ______________ by graduate students at Cambridge University.
5. The rules are pretty ______________: You take turns moving pieces until you capture the opponent's king.
6. If you're not getting enough vitamins in your diet, you should take a(n) ______________.
7. ______________ foods, such as the ones you get in fast-food restaurants, contain a lot of chemicals.
8. English words ______________ from Greek or Latin often don't follow English grammar rules.

CRITICAL-THINKING SKILL

Considering Objections

An important part of critical thinking is to consider objections to the author's points. Readers shouldn't immediately accept an author's argument or claims. Objections are ideas, factors, or examples that suggest the author's points are incorrect. For example, an author may state that eating meat is unacceptable because factory farms are cruel to animals. An objection to this point is that not all meat comes from factory farms.

1 Read the excerpt. Evaluate it with a partner and complete the activities.

> Massive amounts of energy are required to provide [farm animals] with shelter, food, and transportation. Also, farm animals, particularly cows, create methane—a greenhouse gas. In the US, it's estimated that agriculture is responsible for ten percent of all emissions.

CONSIDER OBJECTION Based on the information in the excerpt, circle the objection you most agree with.

a. Not all agricultural pollution is directly caused by farm animals.

b. Pollution caused by transportation will be reduced by adopting greener energy systems.

c. Greener alternatives can only be considered if consumers are willing to pay more for meat.

SUMMARIZE Write a short explanation describing why you agree with the objection.

____

2 Read the excerpt. Do you have any objections? Write your answer.

> After becoming vegetarian, many people notice both immediate and long-lasting improvements to their health. Most plant-based diets contain foods that are less processed and have fewer chemicals. Eating more natural and less processed food means you are more likely to have lower blood sugar, which reduces your risk of diabetes.

____

____

IDEAS IN DISCUSSION

1. Discuss the different types of vegetarian diets (lacto-vegetarian, ovo-vegetarian, lacto-ovo vegetarian, pescatarian, vegan, and flexitarian) and the benefits and challenges associated with each. In particular, explore the concept of the flexitarian diet, which includes mostly plant-based foods with occasional consumption of animal products.

2. Discuss the health benefits associated with a plant-based diet, such as lower blood sugar, reduced risk of diabetes, lower cholesterol, and increased intake of antioxidants. Additionally, consider the potential nutritional challenges of a vegetarian diet, such as obtaining complete proteins, vitamin B12, and easily absorbable iron, and how these challenges can be addressed.
3. Explore the various reasons people choose to become vegetarians, including health benefits, environmental impact, religious beliefs, and moral considerations. How do cultural traditions and family practices influence the choice to adopt a vegetarian diet? Can adopting a vegetarian diet have positive effects on mental health and emotional well-being?
4. Analyze how vegetarian diets can positively affect the environment by reducing land use, energy consumption, and greenhouse gas emissions. How do plant-based diets compare to meat-based diets in terms of carbon footprint, water usage, and land use?
5. Debate the ethical considerations surrounding vegetarianism, including animal welfare and the moral implications of consuming animal products. Additionally, discuss the long-term sustainability of vegetarian diets in terms of personal health, environmental impact, and societal change.

IDEAS IN WRITING

1. **Health and Nutrition:** How does a vegetarian diet compare to a traditional omnivorous diet in terms of overall health benefits? How does a plant-based diet contribute to cardiovascular health, and what are the underlying mechanisms? What are the common nutrient deficiencies associated with vegetarian diets, and how can they be addressed?
2. **Environmental Impact:** What is the environmental impact of meat production, and how does it contribute to climate change? How can a shift towards vegetarian diets help reduce greenhouse gas emissions? What is the water footprint of meat production, and how can vegetarianism help conserve water resources?
3. **Ethical Considerations:** What are the ethical arguments for and against meat consumption, and how does vegetarianism align with these principles? How does vegetarianism promote compassion towards animals? How do personal values, beliefs, and ethical considerations influence the decision to adopt a vegetarian diet? What are the religious perspectives on meat consumption, and how do they relate to vegetarianism?
4. **Social and Economic Factors:** How can vegetarianism contribute to addressing food insecurity in developing countries? What is the role of the food industry in promoting plant-based alternatives, and how is this industry evolving? How have social movements influenced the rise of vegetarianism, and what impact have these movements had on societal attitudes? What are the global implications of meat-heavy diets on food security and sustainable food systems?
5. **Cultural and Culinary Aspects:** How do different cultures around the world incorporate vegetarian diets into their traditional cuisines? What are some popular vegetarian dishes from various global cuisines, and how do they reflect cultural practices and values? How have global trends and movements, such as the rise of plant-based diets, shaped the evolution of culinary practices worldwide?

PSYCHOLOGY

UNIT 2-1 Are Geniuses Normal?

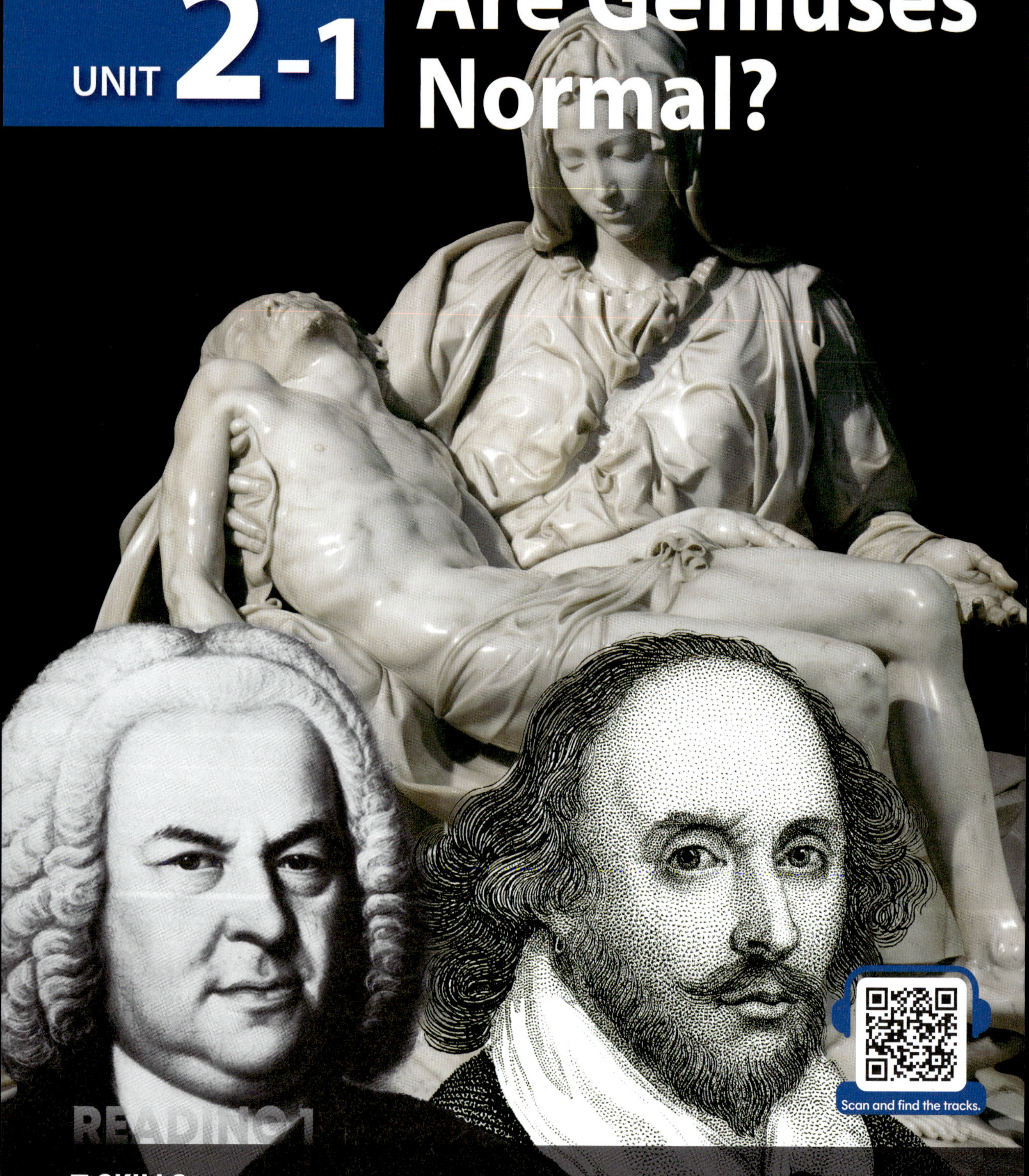

Scan and find the tracks.

READING 1

SKILLS

Reading Skill:
Identifying the Author's Point of View

Critical-Thinking Skill:
Considering Objections

WARM-UP QUESTIONS

1. Who do you consider to be the most creative person in Korea or in history?
2. Why do you believe this?
3. Do you think he or she was inherently different from others?
4. What images come to mind when you think of creative artists, writers, and scientists?
5. What does "being creative" mean to you?
6. What do you know about Steve Jobs, William Shakespeare, and J. S. Bach?
7. Which is more important for achievement: talents or hard work?

BEFORE YOU READ

Read the statements. Check (✓) whether you agree or disagree with each statement. Discuss your answers with a partner.

	Strongly disagree	Disagree somewhat	Agree somewhat	Strongly agree
1. Most intelligent people are a little strange.				
2. The people I admire the most are highly creative.				
3. Business leaders don't need to be creative.				
4. It's hard for the average person to understand great art, music, and literature.				
5. Training and discipline are more important than creativity.				

VOCABULARY PREVIEW

1 Read the sentences. Circle the words closest in meaning to the words in bold.

1. Great creators throughout history are seen as **odd**.
   a. worthy b. challenging c. weird
2. Artists shouldn't be **constrained** by the usual rules of society.
   a. restricted b. represented c. interpreted
3. This view of creativity is common but may not be **accurate**.
   a. proven b. correct c. popular
4. Creative people actually aren't strange **overall**.
   a. in general b. without question c. by themselves
5. Peter Drucker rejects the **label** "creative" and instead prefers to see himself as productive.
   a. goal b. claim c. description
6. The book's **thesis** is that highly creative people are special in some way.
   a. denial b. argument c. implication
7. Many people who were contacted by the author did not **grant** him an interview.
   a. show b. allow c. send
8. Perhaps people can **attain** creativity by developing certain habits.
   a. achieve b. accept c. attempt

2 Match the words in bold in section 1 above to their definitions below.

________ : free from mistakes; correct

________ : to reach to succeed in getting something

________ : to control and limit something

________ : to agree to do, give or allow

________ : a word or a phrase that is used to describe the characteristics or qualities of people, activities, or things, often in a way that is unfair

________ : strange or unexpected

________ : with everyone and everything included; in general

________ : a statement that someone wants to discuss or prove

ARE GENIUSES NORMAL?

Track 03

1. **Reading Skill: Identifying the Author's Point of View**
   A point of view is the attitude or position a person takes on a subject. A neutral point of view doesn't choose sides. A biased point of view is either influenced by outside factors or the writer's opinion.

2. **Critical-Thinking Skill: Considering Objections**
   An important part of critical thinking is considering objections to the author's points. Objections are ideas, factors, or examples that suggest the author's points are incorrect.

Geniuses[1] are kind of odd—or so most people believe. There are stories about great creators throughout history who were more than a little **eccentric**[2]. It is said that Michelangelo seldom bathed or changed his clothes; the poet Lord Byron kept a pet bear in his dorm room at Cambridge University; Nikola Tesla claimed he never slept more than two hours at a time; and Steve Jobs experimented with an all-fruit diet.

Scientific research even confirms that we associate creativity with being different. In one study, two groups looked at photos of a fictional artist and his work. One group was shown an ordinary-looking man in a suit, and the other an unusually dressed man with a strange hairstyle. Although the groups were shown identical works of art, the second group liked the art more. According to the researchers, we expect creative people to be free spirits and not constrained by the standard rules of society. But is this view of creativity accurate?

Despite the colorful tales about historical innovators, there is some reason to believe that creative people are not particularly odd overall. For one thing, many of these stories are **exaggerated**[3] by popular imagination. In fact, it wasn't that unusual for people to bathe rarely during Michelangelo's time, before convenient water supplies and modern **hygiene**[4] standards

1	**genius**	*n.*	someone who is extremely intelligent or extremely good at something
2	**eccentric**	*adj.*	behaving in a strange and unusual way
3	**exaggerate**	*v.*	to make something seem larger, better, worse, etc., than it really is
4	**hygiene**	*n.*	the process of keeping things clean, especially to prevent disease

existed. The "fruitarianism" of Steve Jobs wasn't unique to him but is shared by quite a few vegans (though its health effects are worthy of criticism). And so on.

More importantly, the stereotype of the strange genius doesn't consider the many great creators who followed the rules, both in their work and in life. William Shakespeare is a giant of literature, but he largely followed literary convention in his poems and plays. He also lived a quiet, thoroughly ordinary life with his wife and their three children. Johann Sebastian Bach was another responsible family man who produced immortal works of art—within the fairly rigid musical structures accepted as proper in Germany in the 1700s.

One anecdote illustrates very well how creativity can occur without an eccentric personality behind it. When the psychologist Mihaly Csikszentmihalyi was researching creative people and what they have in common for a book he was writing, one of the innovators with whom he sought an interview was Peter Drucker. A business consultant and author, Drucker is widely considered the founder of modern management theory and education. In his reply, Drucker politely thanked the researcher for **honoring**[5] him with the request before explaining why he couldn't help and why he even rejected the label "creative".

"I am told I am creative — I don't know what that means . . . I hope you will not think me ***presumptuous***[6] *or rude if I say that one of the secrets of productivity (in which I believe, whereas I do not believe in creativity) is to have a VERY BIG* ***wastepaper basket***[7] *to take care of ALL invitations such as yours. "*

Drucker was an original and influential person who clearly disagreed with Csikszentmihalyi's thesis that creativity is an exceptional **trait**[8] or a set of features. He didn't see himself as unique but believed that his achievements resulted from consistent hard effort and, above all, careful use of his time. (Many productive people seem to agree. Out of several hundred invitations to successful artists, writers, scientists, and other achievers sent by Csikszentmihalyi, only ninety- one people took the time to grant him an interview.)

In a way, this is a more attractive concept of creativity than the popular idea of the genius as a troubled rebel. Maybe creativity isn't a rare personality trait that we are or aren't born with but something we might all be able to attain through conscious effort and good habits. What could be more normal than that?

5	**honor**	*v.*	to show great respect for someone or something
6	**presumptuous**	*adj.*	failing to act within the limits of what is allowed or appropriate
7	**wastepaper basket**	*n.*	an open container for putting trash in, especially paper
8	**trait**	*n.*	a particular characteristic that can produce a particular type of behavior

COMPREHENSION CHECK-UPS

1. What is the main idea of the reading? What are the key points or arguments presented?

2. In paragraph 1, what might be wrong with the argument that geniuses are odd? Think of at least one objection.

3. According to paragraph 2, which is true about the study?

a. Two groups looked at pictures of actual artists.
b. One of the two artists was wearing a suit.
c. Each group was shown a different artwork.
d. People liked the normal-looking artist's work better.

4. According to paragraph 2, what was the conclusion of the study?

a. You can often tell if a person is creative by their appearance.
b. Ordinary people are not very good judges of artistic quality.
c. Unusual-looking people produce higher-quality art.
d. People tend to see nonconformists as more creative.

5. Which of the following is NOT stated in paragraph 3?

a. The popular view of creativity could be incorrect.
b. Stories about famous people from the past are unreliable.
c. Today's hygiene standards did not apply in Michelangelo's time.
d. Steve Jobs denied reports that he practiced "fruitarianism."

6. What can be inferred from paragraph 3?

a. The majority of stories and beliefs about Michelangelo are incorrect.

b. Michelangelo's behavior was highly unusual for his time.

c. Stories about eccentric creators are popular among ordinary people.

d. An all-fruit diet is common among famous creators.

7. In paragraph 4, why does the author mention William Shakespeare?

a. To contrast his life with that of Johann Sebastian Bach

b. To give an example of a genius who was not eccentric

c. To show that popular ideas about great artists are mostly accurate

d. To illustrate that the world's greatest writers do not obey the rules

8. According to paragraph 5, which is true of Peter Drucker?

a. He was generally considered to be eccentric.

b. He turned down a request to be Csikszentmihalyi's co-author.

c. He is an influential figure in the field of business management.

d. He explained his view of creativity in an interview with Csikszentmihalyi.

9. According to paragraph 7, how did Peter Drucker describe himself?

a. Not creative but productive

b. Not unique but creative

c. Not hard-working but high-achieving

d. Not influential but exceptional

10. In paragraph 8, what concept of creativity is the author describing as "more attractive"?

____

____

MAPPING IDEAS

Read the statements and match them to the people whose opinions are stated in the reading.

1. Geniuses are kind of odd . . .
   a. historians　　b. psychologists　　c. the average person　　d. the author

2. [People] expect creative people to be free spirits and not constrained by the standard rules of society.
   a. researchers　　b. study participants　　c. artists　　d. the author

3. The stereotype of the strange genius doesn't consider the many great creators who followed the rules, . . .
   a. the average person　　b. the author　　c. composers　　d. artists

4. . . . I say that one of the secrets of productivity (in which I believe, whereas I do not believe in creativity) is to have a very big wastepaper basket to take care of all invitations such as yours.
   a. the author　　b. an artist　　c. a business consultant　　d. a psychologist

5. Maybe creativity isn't a rare personality trait that we either are or aren't born with, . . .
   a. the author　　b. a psychologist　　c. a scientist　　d. an artist

VOCABULARY REVIEW

Fill in the blanks with the correct words from the box. Change the form if needed.

thesis	exaggerate	grant	trait
constrain	label	attain	presumptuous

1. The movies mix drama, comedy, and horror, so it's hard to put a(n) ______________ on them.
2. Usually, you should clearly state the ______________ of your essay in the introduction.
3. Both our physical characteristics and our personality ______________ are affected by genes.
4. Evan claims that he hasn't slept at all for three nights straight, but I think he must be ______________.
5. The law is meant to ______________ big corporations so that they don't become too powerful.
6. It's very ______________ for a student to offer advice to a professor on how to teach.
7. Before a child can receive this medical treatment, a parent has to ______________ permission.
8. My goal is to ______________ a high-level management position by the time I'm thirty.

CRITICAL-THINKING SKILL

Considering Objections

An important part of critical thinking is to consider objections to the author's points. Readers shouldn't immediately accept an author's argument or claims. Objections are ideas, factors, or examples that suggest the author's points are incorrect. For example, an author may state that eating meat is unacceptable because factory farms are cruel to animals. An objection to this point is that not all meat comes from factory farms.

1 Read the excerpt. Evaluate it with a partner and complete the activities.

More importantly, the stereotype of the strange genius doesn't consider the many great creators who followed the rules, both in their work and in life. William Shakespeare is a giant of literature, but he largely followed literary convention in his poems and plays. He also lived a quiet, thoroughly ordinary life with his wife and their three children.

CONSIDER Based on the information in the excerpt, circle the objection you most agree with.

OBJECTION

a. Shakespeare used known literary forms but was original in his style and use of language.

b. We actually don't know much for sure about Shakespeare's life. It might have been much less conventional than we think.

c. Some experts say that the person we know as "Shakespeare" wasn't the real author. The actual author may have been an eccentric person who didn't want to be identified.

SUMMARIZE Write a short explanation describing why you agree with the objection.

____

2 Share one opinion you usually hold about people, things, or situations based on your personal experience. (student A)

____

3 Read your partner's opinion and provide a well-reasoned objection. (student B)

____

IDEAS IN DISCUSSION

1. What other words might describe someone who is "eccentric"?
   In what ways can people express eccentricity? How might our cultural background shape our understanding of what it means to be "eccentric"?
2. Do you think creativity and eccentricity are connected?
   If so, how might they interact or influence each other?
   Is eccentricity a necessary component of creativity?
3. Is being a genius the same as being creative, or are they distinct?
   How do societal expectations and stereotypes about genius and creativity shape our views of these concepts?
   Is one essential for the other?
4. Consider people in your life who are notably creative or eccentric.
   How do you view them differently? Do their distinctive qualities make them more inspiring, challenging, or memorable?
   How do cultural and societal norms shape our views of creativity and eccentricity?
5. Besides those mentioned in the reading, who are some well-known geniuses—real or fictional—known for their "odd" behavior?
   What effect do you think their eccentricities have had on their work, public image, or legacy?

IDEAS IN WRITING

1. **Challenge the Stereotype of the "Eccentric Genius"**
   Write an essay discussing whether creativity requires an "odd" personality. Do you agree with the author's view? Use examples from the reading or personal experiences to support your position.
2. **Define and Reflect on "Creativity"**
   How do you define creativity? Is it an inborn trait, a skill to develop, or both? Discuss how Drucker's view on creativity shapes your definition.
3. **Reflect on Skill Improvement**
   Think of a skill you improved through consistent effort. How does your experience support or challenge the article's view that anyone can become creative with effort and good habits?
4. **Profile a "Creative" Person You Admire**
   Choose a creative person you admire and describe their personality and habits. Do they fit the "eccentric genius" stereotype or resemble Drucker's approach? How does this influence your view of creativity?
5. **Explain Why Creativity Matters in Your Life**
   Write about how creativity has impacted your life in school, work, or hobbies. Do you consider yourself naturally creative, or is it something you've developed over time?

PSYCHOLOGY

UNIT 2-2 Hooray for Pessimism!

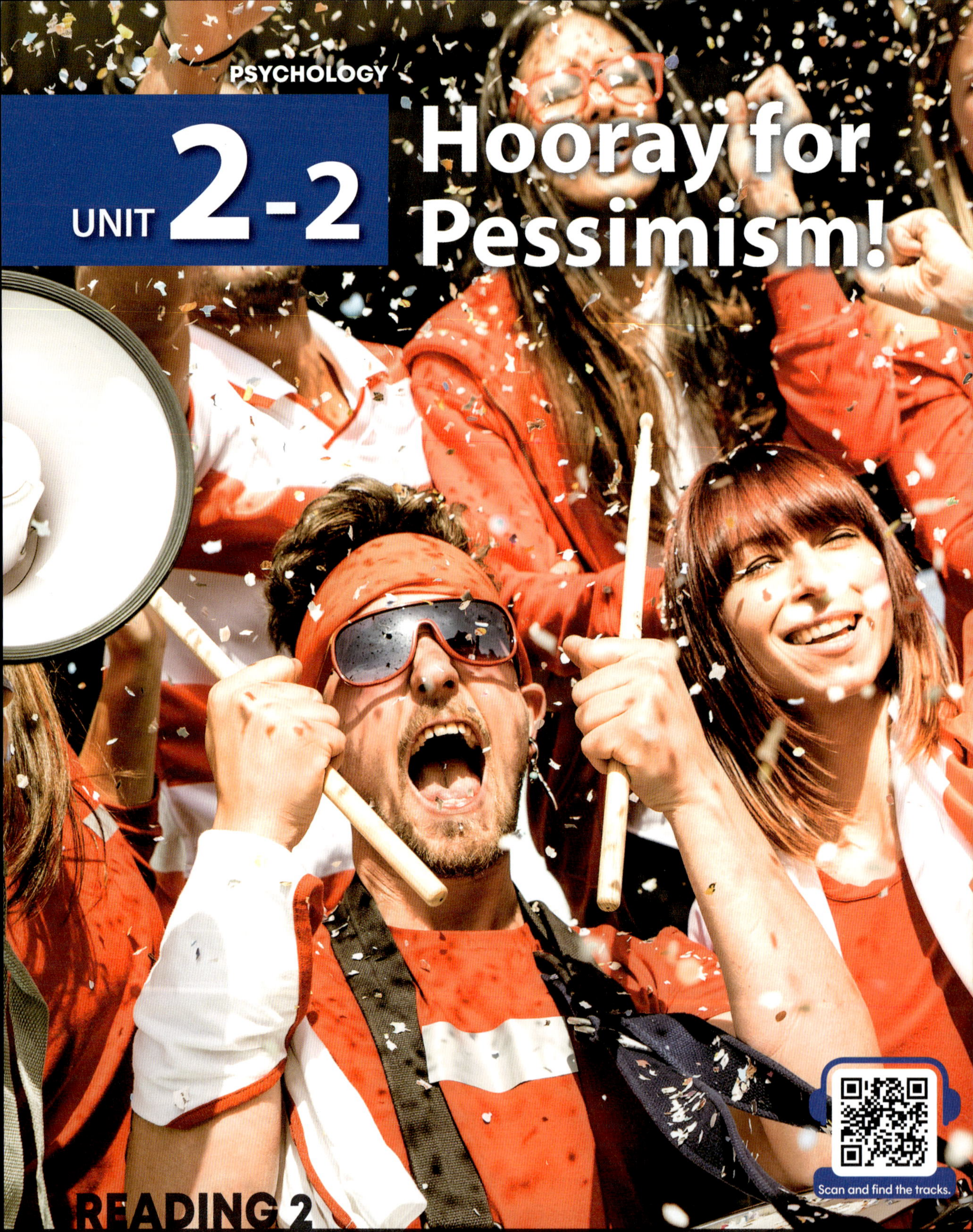

Scan and find the tracks.

READING 2

SKILLS

Reading Skill:
Clarifying Understanding

Critical-Thinking Skill:
Detecting Irrelevant Points

WARM-UP QUESTIONS

1. When is it good to be an optimist? What risks might come with positive thinking?
2. When is it beneficial to have a pessimistic outlook, and why might pessimism sometimes be advantageous?
3. What are some common misconceptions about pessimists and optimists?
4. What strategies do you use to manage your emotions in challenging situations?
5. Can pessimism, often unfairly maligned, offer significant advantages in various aspects of life, from personal relationships to professional success?

BEFORE YOU READ

Read the statements. Check (✓) whether you agree or disagree with each statement. Discuss your answers with a partner.

	Strongly disagree	Disagree somewhat	Agree somewhat	Strongly agree
1. I don't mind people with pessimistic personalities.				
2. I think a person can be too optimistic.				
3. I dislike it when people tell me to "cheer up."				
4. I think it's important to always have a plan B.				
5. I think it's best to always expect the worst.				

VOCABULARY PREVIEW

1 Read the sentences. Circle the words closest in meaning to the words in bold.

1. The advantages of optimism **notwithstanding**, I think pessimism also has many benefits.
   a. around　　b. considered　　c. aside

2. In relationships, pessimistic **partners** are less likely to be disappointed by difficulties.
   a. companions　　b. compatriots　　c. communities

3. According to one expert, pessimism also **confers** advantages in our working lives.
   a. submits　　b. grants　　c. insists

4. If an optimist is **denied** a job they expect to get, they will be very disappointed.
   a. allocated　　b. drafted　　c. refused

5. In similar circumstances, a pessimist will be less negatively **affected** as they expect less.
   a. impacted　　b. retracted　　c. anticipated

6. Defensive pessimism means that people work hard to avoid major and **minor** problems.
   a. trivial　　b. permissive　　c. ongoing

7. Defensive pessimism is the tendency to think that anything could go wrong and use it as **motivation** to act.
   a. mobility　　b. persuasion　　c. encouragement

8. Given its ability to prepare us for the worst, it is surprising that pessimism is not seen as a **valid** outlook.
   a. contemporary　　b. reasonable　　c. inclusive

2 Match the words in bold in section 1 above to their definitions below.

________ : to act on and cause a change in someone or something

________ : to give something, such as a degree, award, title, right, etc. to someone or something

________ : to refuse to give

________ : inferior in importance, size, or degree; comparatively unimportant

________ : a force or influence that causes someone to do something

________ : despite; regardless

________ : someone's husband or wife or the person someone has sexual relations with

________ : fair, reasonable, or acceptable

HOORAY FOR PESSIMISM!

Track 04

1. Reading Skill: Clarifying Understanding

You can take steps to clarify anything you do not understand. For example, re-read parts of a text, guess the meaning of unfamiliar words, explain something in your own words, try to visualize the text, etc.

2. Critical-Thinking Skill: Detecting Irrelevant Points

Writers sometimes use irrelevant points to confuse readers, take attention away from the main topic, or make an argument seem stronger than it really is. Read carefully to avoid being tricked by irrelevant information.

"Think positive!" "Look on the bright side!" These words of advice—commands, really—regularly come my way from family, friends, co-workers, and even total strangers. However, these empty statements do little to ease my anxieties because, deep down, I consider myself a pessimist. That's not to say that I'm unhappy. However, at any given moment, I'm likely to be preoccupied with scenarios about what might go wrong next. The social and health benefits of optimism notwithstanding, I've learned that pessimism is greatly **underrated**[1], and a healthy amount of such negativity can benefit a person emotionally, professionally, and financially.

Pessimism takes many forms, but the relevant ones here are **dispositional**[2] and defensive pessimism. In psychology, dispositional pessimism is the personality trait of having generally low expectations. In other words, dispositional pessimists may not know what will happen, but they are pretty sure it won't be anything great.

Although this sounds like a **dreary**[3] way to go through life, surprisingly, dispositional pessimism might lead to stronger, longer-lasting relationships. Several studies have found that negativity positively affects a couple because it prepares them for the worst. One study followed eighty-two married couples and found that the optimists suffered most because of their "extreme and often irrational" disappointment when they encountered difficulties. In contrast, dispositional pessimists

1 **underrated** *adj.* not valued enough
2 **dispositional** *adv.* related to the tendency of how one acts or thinks
3 **dreary** *adj.* depressing

accepted some trouble with their partners as normal and could thus deal with it better.

A bit of dispositional pessimism confers some advantages at work as well, according to psychologist and critic of what he calls the "**cult**[4]" of optimism, Dr. Aaron Sackett. As he explained to *Psychology Today*, if an optimist is denied an expected promotion, they will feel both shocked and crushed. However, a pessimist in the same situation never **had his or her hopes up**[5] to begin with, so he or she will not be nearly so deeply affected. "Optimists never get the joy of a pleasant surprise," Sackett points out. While that sounds like a **bummer**[6], this mentality can be beneficial in helping pessimists move on and focus on what lies ahead.

Defensive pessimism, which some could view as dispositional pessimism applied to specific situations, can benefit people in more **concrete**[7] ways. Defensive pessimism can be described as the tendency to be anxious about all the things that could go wrong, both major and minor, and to use that anxiety as motivation to act. Imagine you are a pessimist in charge of organizing an important presentation. You might expect technical problems, so you'll set up and test the computer equipment in advance. And you may fear that additional people might show up, so you'll have extra copies of the handouts ready. Through the power of negative thinking, you will be much better prepared than the optimist that assumes everything will proceed smoothly.

Defensive pessimism may also lead to more **prudent**[8] money management. One interesting experiment involved observing college students gambling on simulated card games and slot machines. Those who had scored high on a test of optimism were more likely to believe they would win—and they believed this even more strongly after they had lost money, leading to further losses. Only the pessimistic students reduced their bets after losing, which is surely the logical thing to do. A similar principle could be observed on a global scale following the 2008 world financial crisis, which made defensive pessimists out of millions of people. Since then, many of those in affected countries have felt increased anxiety about their financial futures and have adjusted their behavior accordingly, saving more for retirement and avoiding disastrous credit card debt.

Considering how pessimism can prevent disappointment, **shield**[9] one's ego, and protect against job-related or financial misfortunes, one would think it would be more widely accepted as a valid point of view. Dr. Julie Norem, who specializes in this area, told the *Huffington Post*: "Currently, there's an awful lot of pressure for people to present themselves as cheery and optimistic, and it probably causes more pain than pessimism itself." Norem adds that the dominance of optimism may be coming to an end, and soon there may be a "broad cultural shift" toward more negativity. Maybe, but I'm not getting my hopes up.

4	**cult**	*n.*	a misplaced or excessive admiration for a particular person or thing
5	**get/have one's hopes up**	*idiom*	to become hopeful
6	**bummer**	*n.*	(*informal*) a thing that is annoying or disappointing
7	**concrete**	*adj.*	involving specific people, situations, etc., and not ideas or qualities
8	**prudent**	*adj.*	careful and sensible
9	**shield**	*v.*	to protect

COMPREHENSION CHECK-UPS

1. **Which of the following best describes the author's personality, according to paragraph 1?**

a. He or she focuses on negative possibilities.

b. He or she worries about being a pessimist.

c. He or she wishes they were an optimist.

d. He or she listens to the advice of others.

2. **Which of the following is stated in paragraph 3?**

a. Pessimists should avoid dating optimists.

b. Optimists' relationships usually last longer.

c. Pessimists handle hard times more effectively.

d. Optimists become reasonably disappointed by failure.

3. **According to paragraph 4, which is NOT true of people's relationship with work?**

a. Failure to get a promotion or a new job will have a worse effect on pessimists.

b. Those who expect to succeed miss out on feelings of unexpected happiness.

c. Dr. Sackett believes that thinking too positively is a dangerous phenomenon.

d. People who think they are likely to be successful often encounter trauma.

4. **According to paragraph 5, all of the following are true EXCEPT _______.**

a. defensive pessimism can ensure that we have considered all eventualities

b. defensive pessimism is used more actively than dispositional pessimism

c. dispositional pessimism is best used to plan for minor issues that cause anxiety

d. dispositional pessimism has fewer practical advantages than defensive pessimism

5. **Read paragraph 5. Explain what defensive pessimism is.**

____

____

6. Which of the following is stated in paragraph 6?

a. Scientists investigated what attracts college students to gambling.
b. The more optimistic students found gambling more enjoyable.
c. Optimists in the study were more likely to lose their bets.
d. Pessimistic students took smaller risks after experiencing losses.

7. Which statement best restates the sentence, "A similar principle could be observed on a global scale following the 2008 world financial crisis, which made defensive pessimists out of millions of people." from paragraph 6?

a. The 2008 financial crisis made pessimists more anxious.
b. In 2008, optimists made more money than pessimists.
c. The financial crash in 2008 made people more cautious.
d. Pessimists lost more money than optimists did in 2008.

8. Read paragraph 6. Explain how defensive pessimism has changed the behavior after the financial crisis.

____

____

9. What can be inferred from paragraph 6?

a. Students are at extra risk of gambling addiction.
b. The financial crisis was mostly caused by pessimists.
c. Gambling is a very dangerous pastime for pessimists.
d. Optimists are at greater risk of losing money while gambling.

10. In paragraph 7, why does the author use the phrase "broad cultural shift"?

a. To describe how optimism is growing in strength
b. To suggest that pessimism will become deeply unfashionable
c. To explain how pressure makes society cheerier and more optimistic
d. To suggest that the age of optimism may soon be over

MAPPING IDEAS

Read the sentences from the reading and match them with the summary sentences that share the same meaning.

HOORAY FOR PESSIMISM!		
ORIGINAL SENTENCES		**SUMMARY SENTENCES**
1. "Think positive!""Look on the bright side!". . . [T]hese empty statements do little to ease my anxieties because, deep down, I consider myself a pessimist.	___	a. Optimists suffer more in failed relationships because they expect too much from their partners.
2. [D]ispositional pessimism is the personality trait of having generally low expectations. In other words, dispositional pessimists may not know what will happen, but they are pretty sure it won't be anything great.	___	b. An experiment found that optimists tend to make riskier choices when gambling.
3. One study followed eighty-two married couples and found that the optimists suffered most because of their "extreme and often irrational"disappointment when they encountered difficulties.	___	c. It's hard for pessimists to feel at ease simply by the commands of others to be positive.
4. Defensive pessimism, which some could view as dispositional pessimism applied to specific situations, can benefit people in more concrete ways.	___	d. Dispositional pessimism is a state where people have low expectations and expect the worst.
5. One interesting experiment involved observing college students gambling on simulated card games and slot machines. Those who had scored high on a test of optimism were more likely to believe they would win, . . . leading to further losses.	___	e. One type of pessimism can be used in practically helpful ways.

VOCABULARY REVIEW

Fill in the blanks with the correct words from the box. Change the form if needed.

notwithstanding	affect	deny	minor
partner	valid	dreary	cult

1. Alan's new passport is ________________ until June 2031.
2. The planting of new trees ________________, the rainforest is still being rapidly destroyed.
3. Helen had a(n) ________________ injury while playing soccer. She sprained her ankle.
4. The suspect being questioned by police strongly ________________ stealing anything.
5. It was a wet and ________________ Wednesday afternoon, so the children played inside.
6. The media referred to the charismatic CEO's followers as his ________________.
7. When you get married, you agree to accept the other as your lifelong ________________.
8. While it did not collapse, the strength of the building was badly ________________ by the earthquake.

CRITICAL-THINKING SKILL

Detecting Irrelevant Points

Writers sometimes use irrelevant points to confuse readers, take attention away from the main topic, or make an argument seem stronger than it really is. Careful readers can distinguish points that are related to the argument and those that are not. By ignoring irrelevant points, readers can avoid being distracted and focus on evaluating the writer's main argument. For example:

(1) Violent crime is common in areas where people have easy access to guns.

(2) The US has more guns per person than any other nation.

(3) Therefore, the government should make it more difficult for people to buy guns.

Statement 2 is related to the topic; however, the conclusion (statement 3) doesn't follow from it.

1 **Read the excerpt. Evaluate it with a partner and complete the activities.**

MAIN IDEA OF PARAGRAPH 3 *Pessimists deal with disappointment better.*

(1) Although this sounds like a dreary way to go through life, surprisingly, dispositional pessimism might lead to stronger, longer-lasting relationships. **(2)** Several studies have found that negativity positively affects a couple because it prepares them for the worst. One study followed eighty-two married couples and found that the optimists suffered most because of their "extreme and often irrational" disappointment when they encountered difficulties. In contrast, dispositional pessimists accepted some trouble with their partners as normal and could thus deal with it better.

Is part (1) relevant to the main idea of the paragraph? ☐ Yes ☐ No

Is part (2) relevant to the main idea of the paragraph? ☐ Yes ☐ No

2 **Summarize the excerpt.**

____

____

IDEAS IN DISCUSSION

1. Weigh the pros and cons of both optimistic and pessimistic outlooks. Which outlook do you believe is ultimately more beneficial? Discuss how pessimism can be beneficial emotionally, professionally, and financially. Consider examples from the article and your own experiences.
2. Compare and contrast dispositional pessimism and defensive pessimism, and explore how each can affect various aspects of life, such as relationships and work. Argue the practicality

of defensive pessimism in everyday life, providing examples of how anticipating negative outcomes can lead to better preparedness and outcomes.

3. Analyze how pessimism is perceived in contemporary culture and discuss the potential benefits and drawbacks of adopting a pessimistic outlook. Evaluate the ethical implications of society's emphasis on optimism, considering the potential harm it may cause to individuals who do not naturally align with this outlook.
4. Explore the concept of ego protection in pessimists compared to optimists. How does having lower expectations help in dealing with disappointments? Evaluate the claim that pessimism can lead to stronger, longer-lasting relationships. Use examples from the article and additional research to support your argument.
5. Debate the societal pressure to be optimistic and how this might impact individuals who naturally lean towards pessimism. How might the historical and philosophical backgrounds of Confucianism and Christianity lead to differing views on the role of pessimism in personal and societal development?

IDEAS IN WRITING

1. **The Benefits of Pessimism:** How does pessimism protect individuals from disappointment and emotional pain? Can a healthy dose of pessimism lead to better decision-making and risk management? How can pessimists balance their negative outlook with a positive approach to life?
2. **The Cultural Bias Towards Optimism:** Why is optimism so widely celebrated in our society? Examine societal pressures to be optimistic and the potential negative consequences of suppressing natural pessimistic tendencies. How does this cultural bias affect individuals who naturally lean towards pessimism? Can we create a more balanced and acceptable view of different personality traits?
3. **Pessimism in Relationships:** How can pessimism contribute to stronger and more resilient relationships? How can couples with different perspectives on optimism and pessimism find common ground? What are the potential drawbacks of excessive optimism in relationships?
4. **Pessimism in the Workplace and Financial Management:** Analyze how pessimism can be an asset in professional settings, particularly in terms of preparation and expectation management. How can employers and managers create a work environment that values both optimism and pessimism? Explore how a pessimistic mindset can promote prudent financial behavior, such as saving, investing wisely, and avoiding risky ventures. How can defensive pessimism lead to more prudent financial decisions?
5. **The Future of Pessimism:** Will there be a shift towards greater acceptance of pessimism in the future? How can we challenge the negative stereotypes associated with pessimism? Can we learn to appreciate the value of a balanced perspective that incorporates both optimism and pessimism? By challenging societal norms that glorify optimism, can we embrace the benefits of pessimism and foster a more nuanced understanding of human behavior?

SCIENCE & MEDICINE

UNIT 3-1 First Line of Defense

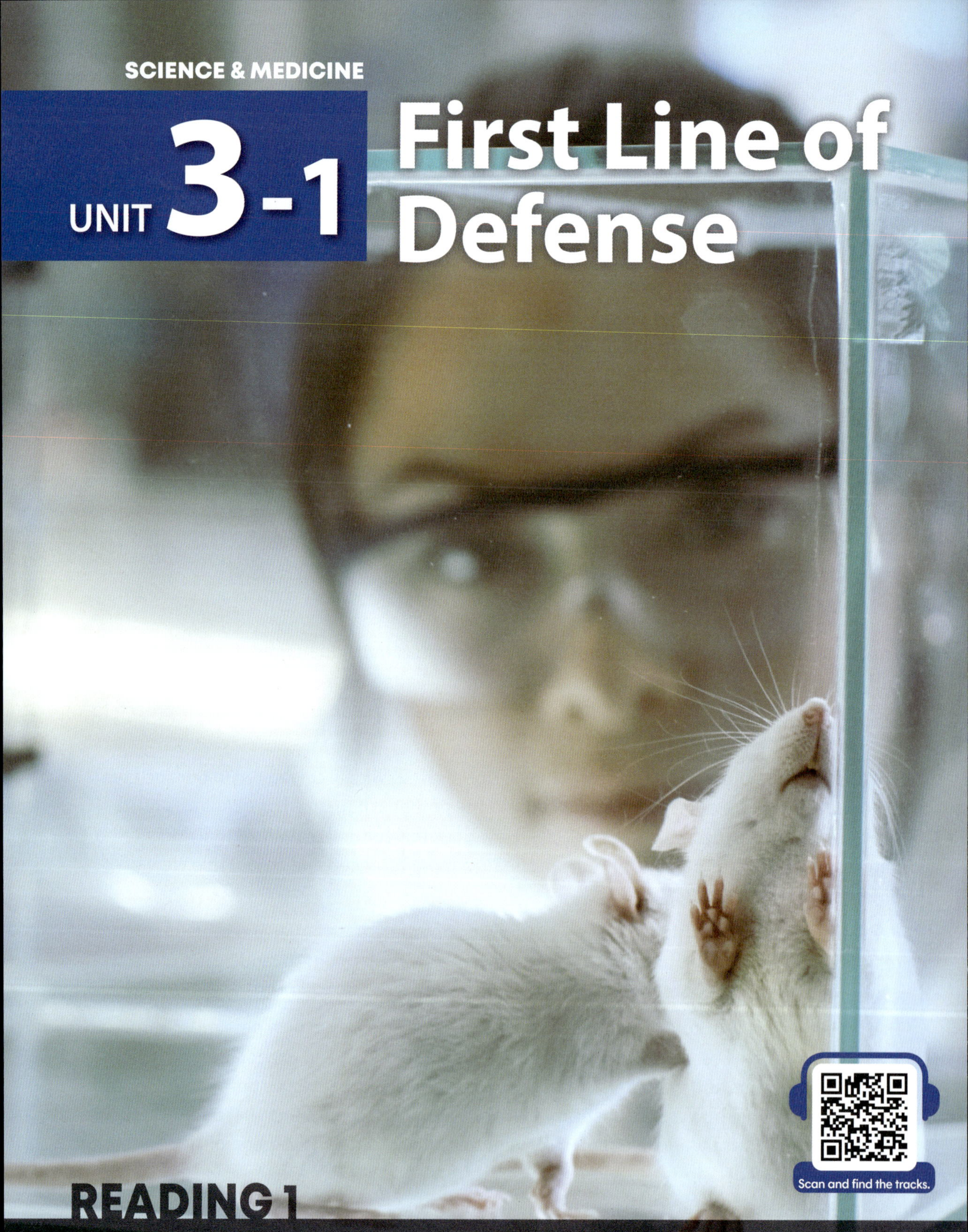

Scan and find the tracks.

READING 1

SKILLS

Reading Skill:
Extracting and Recalling Information

Critical-Thinking Skill:
Classifying Statements

WARM-UP QUESTIONS

1. What laws exist in your country that cover the treatment of animals?
2. Is it possible to change people's minds about controversial topics such as animal research?
3. How can scientists balance the need for animal research while ensuring animal welfare?
4. Imagine scientists discover a species with an incredible ability to heal wounds instantly. How could this be applied to human medicine?
5. Can you recall when your immune system successfully fought off an illness? How did you recover?

BEFORE YOU READ

Read the statements. Check (✓) whether you agree or disagree with each statement. Discuss your answers with a partner.

	Strongly disagree	Disagree somewhat	Agree somewhat	Strongly agree
1. I think animal testing is an unavoidable practice.				
2. I think animals and humans should be treated in the same way.				
3. I think animal testing should be limited to small animals.				
4. I think animal testing isn't as helpful as people assume.				
5. I think the use of animals for non-medical experiments should be banned.				

VOCABULARY PREVIEW

1 Read the sentences. Circle the words closest in meaning to the words in bold.

1. Animal testing can be a **controversial** topic.
   a. permanent b. interesting c. difficult

2. **Empirical** evidence shows that animal research is essential.
   a. theoretical b. sensitive c. observed

3. Animals' **internal** makeups are very similar to those of humans.
   a. insecure b. inner c. inferior

4. We need animals because technology cannot **simulate** human systems.
   a. copy b. repair c. study

5. **Preliminary** research using animals helped to create a vaccine for the virus that causes COVID-19.
   a. serious b. detailed c. early

6. There are many **philosophical** arguments about animal research.
   a. clever b. ethical c. social

7. Some believe we should **acknowledge** the rights of animals.
   a. define b. recognize c. research

8. UK **legislation** allows for animal research when there is no other choice.
   a. law b. leader c. politician

2 Match the words in bold in section 1 above to their definitions below.

________ : to accept, admit, or recognize something

________ : causing disagreement or discussion

________ : based on what is experienced or seen rather than on theory

________ : inside the body

________ : a law or set of laws suggested by a government and made official

________ : relating to the study of such things as the nature of the real world or right and wrong

________ : coming before and usually introductory to a certain action or event

________ : to create conditions or processes similar to something that exists

FIRST LINE OF DEFENSE

Track 05

1. **Reading Skill: Extracting and Recalling Information**
   Readers can recall important information by skimming the text. Search for keywords, phrases, dates, or numbers to find information quickly.

2. **Critical-Thinking Skill: Classifying Statements**
   Statements can be classified by the kind of assertion they make. For example, there are predictions, definitions, value judgments, etc. Classifying statements will help you analyze arguments.

Today, in research laboratories across the planet, scientists are working to better understand how diseases behave and how our bodies work by testing chemicals, drugs, and procedures on animals before they are used by or on humans. For some, animal research is a highly controversial practice, but empirical evidence proves that it does not happen without logic or purpose.

Let us begin by examining some of the practical reasons why humans use animals for research. First, animals' internal systems often share similarities with our own: this includes **respiratory**[1], **circulatory**[2], **digestive**[3], nervous, and immune systems. Although science can do many things, these systems are not yet possible to simulate using artificial technologies. However, mice—the animal most often used for research—are a ninety-seven percent genetic match with humans. Furthermore, as most animals have short lives and reproduce quickly, we can study them throughout their lifespan and see the effects of treatments on their next generation.

Another consequence of sharing similarities is that diseases that occur in humans are also very common among animals. Dogs, for example, naturally suffer from cancer, **cataracts**[4], and ulcers (a common stomach complaint). Meanwhile, rabbits are vulnerable to many of the heart conditions that humans can develop, such as blocked **arteries**[5]. Animals can also develop diseases like the

1 **respiratory system** *n.* the system which allows us to breathe oxygen
2 **circulatory system** *n.* the system which pumps blood around our bodies
3 **digestive system** *n.* the system which allows our bodies to digest, or use, food
4 **cataracts** *n.* a disease in which someone's eyes become less clear so that they cannot see clearly
5 **artery** *n.* a thick tube that carries blood from the heart to other parts of the body

flu, and as is well known, COVID-19 seems likely to have begun within bats. In fact, it was due to preliminary research using animals—including mice and monkeys—that scientists were able to develop a human vaccine for the COVID-19 virus so quickly.

Animals have also helped us to better understand our bodies and develop state-of-the-art medical procedures. Much of what we know about the mysteries of the human brain is a result of studying neurotransmitters in giant **squid**[6] and tiny worms called nematodes. These studies have allowed us to expand our understanding of problems such as memory loss. In addition, operations for people that are considered common today were first performed on animals. Hip and knee replacement surgeries were first performed on animals in nineteenth-century Germany by Dr. Themistocles Gluck. In the 1950s, the first successful heart operations and **transplants**[7] were carried out by US doctor John Gibbon—on dogs. Within a few years, Gibbon used what he had learned to save the life of an eighteen-year-old girl with a heart problem. She made a complete recovery and went on to live a long life.

So, without question, animal research educates us and saves human lives, but does that necessarily make it right? To answer this, we need to examine some philosophical arguments about animal research. In 1975, Australian philosopher Peter Singer's influential book *Animal Liberation* was one of the first to make the case against animal testing, painting it as cruel and unnecessary. Singer suggested that we should acknowledge animals as our equals. This point of view, however, leads to an interesting question regarding what is good or bad: would it be right to hurt or even kill one human to save one million human lives? Then, how about one animal? Those opposed to animal research often seem to avoid this difficult question.

Despite the lack of conclusive answers to animal testing's ethical problems, many of the systems we have in place ensure that animal research is as limited and painless as possible. For example, in the UK and the EU, there is legislation that states that animals can only be used for research when it can be proven that there are absolutely no alternatives. Testing on isolated cells and tissues should always be considered first. When there are no other options, the animals being experimented on should be as small as possible: worms or flies, for example. And if it is thought that an animal might suffer, **anesthetics**[8] are legally required.

While it is a topic that people often respond to emotionally, it is important to understand the logic that informs animal research. As we have seen, it has a range of significant benefits, and humans do not experiment on animals simply because they can or because they enjoy it, but because to not do so would lead to greater, more long-term suffering.

[6] **squid** *n.* a sea creature with a long body, eight arms, and two tentacles situated around the mouth
[7] **transplant** *n.* a medical operation in which new organs are put into peoples' bodies
[8] **anesthetic** *n.* a substance that makes people or animals unable to feel pain

COMPREHENSION CHECK-UPS

1. According to paragraph 2, animals are useful for research for all of the following reasons EXCEPT ________.

   a. they are genetically very similar to humans
   b. their systems are very close to those of humans
   c. they can be reproduced using technology
   d. their lives are short, and they reproduce quickly

2. According to paragraph 3, which of the following is NOT true?

   a. Dogs can develop cataracts and stomach problems.
   b. Animals can get cancer, eye problems, and the flu.
   c. Rabbits can develop heart problems, like humans.
   d. Bats were used to develop the COVID-19 vaccine.

3. Read paragraph 3 and name three animals that are mentioned in relation to a global pandemic.

   ____

   ____

4. According to paragraph 4, what development occurred in the middle of the twentieth century?

   a. A doctor found that squid brains were very similar to human brains.
   b. An American doctor successfully replaced a dog's hips and knees.
   c. A German doctor created a breakthrough in hip and knee replacement surgery.
   d. A doctor used his research on dogs to treat a human heart problem.

5. Read paragraph 4. Why are squid mentioned?

   ____

   ____

6 **According to paragraph 5, what argument does Peter Singer's book make?**

a. It could be worth losing some animals to save human lives.

b. Harming an animal is just as bad as harming a human.

c. Animals and humans are not the same, so they cannot be compared.

d. One human life is more valuable than one animal's life.

7. **In paragraph 5, why does the author use the phrase "painting it as cruel and unnecessary"?**

a. To suggest that people use images to question animal research

b. To imply that people describe animal research as a dangerous thing

c. To show arguments that try to make animal research look better

d. To describe how Singer's book tries to convince others about animal testing

8. **According to paragraph 6, what do laws in the EU and UK say?**

a. Animal research should only be done when anesthetics are used.

b. Scientists should use isolated cells, tissues, and organs first.

c. Animal research should be done on worms before other small creatures.

d. Animals in pain should be used for research before healthy animals.

9. **What can be inferred from paragraph 6?**

a. Governments do not trust scientists to regulate testing on their own.

b. Using cells and organs is not as accurate as testing on animals.

c. Unlike larger animals, smaller creatures do not feel pain.

d. People worry that anesthetics do not work on larger animals.

10. **Which statement best restates the sentence, "While it is a topic that people often respond to emotionally, it is important to understand the logic that informs animal research." from paragraph 7?**

a. People get emotional about animal research because of their love of animals.

b. People often forget that animals do not have the same emotions as humans.

c. People get upset about animal research but should know the reasons behind it.

d. People shouldn't feel upset about animal research since it's so helpful.

MAPPING IDEAS

Read the opening sentences from the reading and match them to the correct detail sentences below.

FIRST LINE OF DEFENSE		
PARAGRAPH #	**OPENING SENTENCES**	**DETAILS**
Paragraph 2	Let us begin by examining some of the practical reasons why humans use animals for research.	**1.** ______
Paragraph 3	Another consequence of sharing similarities is that diseases that occur in humans are also very common among animals.	**2.** ______
Paragraph 4	Animals have also helped us to better understand our bodies and develop state-of-the-art medical procedures.	**3.** ______
Paragraph 5	So, without question, animal research educates us and saves human lives, but does that necessarily make it right?	**4.** ______
Paragraph 6	Despite the lack of conclusive answers to animal testing's ethical problems, many of the systems we have in place ensure that animal research is as limited and as painless as possible.	**5.** ______
Paragraph 7	While it is a topic that people often respond to emotionally, it is important to understand the logic that informs animal research.	**6.** ______

DETAILS

a. Animals used in research, such as mice, are genetically similar to humans.
b. Operations like hip and knee replacement surgery were first performed on animals in the 1800s.
c. A philosopher wrote a famous book that argued against animal testing as unnecessary and wrong.
d. People test on animals because it benefits human health and prevents a lot of suffering.
e. Humans and animals both suffer from the flu and COVID-19.
f. In some countries, the law states that animals used in testing have to be given anesthetics.

VOCABULARY REVIEW

Fill in the blanks with the correct words from the box. Change the form if needed.

simulate	**controversial**	**empirical**	**internal**
preliminary	**acknowledge**	**transplant**	**anesthetic**

1. Candidates for the job have a(n) ______________ phone interview before the in-person meeting.
2. We should avoid talking about politics or religion at work, as they can be ______________ subjects.
3. Sadly, the artist's talent was not ______________ by most critics during his lifetime.
4. The melting ice caps are ______________ proof that the climate is changing.
5. At my gym, there's a rock-climbing wall that ______________ the steep side of a mountain.
6. A general ______________ puts humans and animals completely to sleep.
7. Dr. Kaufmann will perform three liver ______________ this week.
8. The ______________ workings of a computer are highly complicated.

CRITICAL-THINKING SKILL

Classifying Statements

Sentences can be classified by the kind of statement they make. Recognizing these can help you analyze arguments.

- **Value judgment:** a claim that something is good or bad, right or wrong, desirable or undesirable, etc.
- **Statement of fact:** a statement of information that can be proven either true or false
- **Causal explanation:** a claim about the reason something has happened or is as it is
- **Allegation:** a claim that is made without complete proof, very often blaming or accusing someone
- **Prediction:** a claim that something will happen in the future

1 **Read the excerpts from the reading and write the statement types. Discuss your choices. Answers may vary.**

1. For some, animal research is a highly controversial practice, but empirical evidence proves that it does not happen without logic or purpose.	
2. First, animals' internal systems often share similarities with our own: this includes respiratory, circulatory, digestive, nervous, and immune systems.	
3. In fact, it was due to preliminary research using animals—including mice and monkeys—that scientists were able to develop a human vaccine for the COVID-19 virus so quickly.	
4. Those opposed to animal research often seem to avoid this difficult question.	
5. As we have seen, [animal research] has a range of significant benefits, and humans do not experiment on animals simply because they can or because they enjoy it, but because to not do so would lead to greater, more long-term suffering.	

IDEAS IN DISCUSSION

1. What laws exist in your country that cover the treatment of animals?

2. Is it possible to change people's minds about controversial topics such as animal research?

3. What is your opinion on animal research?

4. What measures should be taken to ensure the ethical treatment of animals used in scientific research?

5. How can public awareness of animal research help improve perceptions of its necessity and ethics?

IDEAS IN WRITING

Reflective Writing

1. Write a paragraph reflecting on the value of animal research. What do you think would happen without it? (From the textbook)
2. Reflect on your own thoughts about animal research in science. Do you see it as necessary, ethical, or controversial? Why?

Analytical Writing

3. Analyze how advancements in alternative methods (e.g., computer models or cell cultures) are impacting the need for animal research.

Opinion Writing

4. Do the benefits of animal research outweigh the ethical concerns? Argue your perspective.

Exploratory Writing

5. Investigate how studying animals' natural behaviors and traits has inspired human technology or innovations.

SCIENCE & MEDICINE

UNIT 3-2 Red Planet Risks

Scan and find the tracks.

READING 2

SKILLS

Reading Skill:
Making Inferences

Critical-Thinking Skill:
Distinguishing Overgeneralizations

WARM-UP QUESTIONS

1. What do you know about Mars?
2. What do you think is good about exploring space?
3. Would you want to travel to Mars?
4. Have you ever heard of "SpaceX"?
5. Do you think there could be living creatures in space? What kind of creatures do you imagine?

BEFORE YOU READ

Below are things humans might want or need in the future. Rank them from 1 (most interesting to you) to 6 (least interesting to you). Discuss your rankings with a partner.

______ A better understanding of the universe

______ Ways to improve life on Earth

______ Knowledge of life on other planets

______ Access to resources from other planets

______ Established places to live on other planets

______ Ways to travel faster in space

VOCABULARY PREVIEW

1 Read the sentences. Circle the words closest in meaning to the words in bold.

1. H.G. Wells's *War of the Worlds* is a **classic** book that describes aliens from Mars attacking Earth.
   a. complicated b. simple c. outstanding

2. Humans living on Mars would signify a thrilling new **paradigm** for humans.
   a. standard b. planet c. journey

3. The spacecraft *Curiosity* will **investigate** one specific area of Mars.
   a. capture b. examine c. inhabit

4. The US government **allocated** $2.7 billion for its *Perseverance* project.
   a. left out b. put aside c. gave in

5. Some reasons for traveling to Mars, like inspiring people, are quite **abstract**.
   a. philosophical b. actual c. perverse

6. Competition for land on Mars could lead to **military** conflicts.
   a. scientific b. futuristic c. armed

7. Companies could **acquire** valuable minerals and materials from Mars.
   a. learn b. get c. bring

8. Supplies of some materials on Earth will soon be **inadequate**.
   a. insufficient b. unimportant c. inconsistent

2 Match the words in bold in section 1 above to their definitions below.

________ : not associated with any specific instance; theoretical

________ : to get something; to come to own something

________ : to divide and give out (something) for a special reason or to particular people, companies, etc.

________ : serving as a standard of excellence; of recognized value

________ : too small in amount

________ : to observe or study by close examination and systematic inquiry

________ : of or relating to soldiers, arms, or war

________ : a set of theories that explain the way a particular subject is understood at a particular time

RED PLANET RISKS

Track 06

1. **Reading Skill: Making Inferences**
   Writers often imply information. The reader uses the information with their knowledge to make an inference. Inferences should not be confused with predictions.

2. **Critical-Thinking Skill: Distinguishing Overgeneralizations**
   An overgeneralization can be misleading and unfair. To avoid this, writers often use qualifying expressions such as *most, some, a few, etc.*

In his classic 1898 science fiction novel, *War of the Worlds*, H.G. Wells imagined creatures from Mars colonizing Earth. Today, though, **spacecraft**[1] from Earth are the ones on Mars, and governments and businesses are making plans for accessing and utilizing the planet's resources. Humans may even settle there before long, creating an exciting new paradigm for human civilization. However, before we reach that point, we must consider the obstacles that must be overcome to colonize the red planet successfully.

The US National Aeronautics and Space Administration (NASA) first sent out spacecraft capable of exploring Mars in 1975. Two *Viking* spacecraft spent eight years looking for signs of life—and found none. However, they sent back enough valuable photos and knowledge to encourage NASA to continue the program. Since then, the agency has landed nine remote-controlled spacecraft on Mars, including *Curiosity* in 2011 and in 2020, *Perseverance*, whose mission was to investigate a single **crater**[2] on the planet.

The US government allocated $2.7 billion to ensure the success of *Perseverance*. The simple fact that it successfully touched down on Mars is no small achievement: of the forty-nine missions sent to Mars, twenty-eight have failed, and four have partly failed. As for the reasons, they're mainly related to Mars's atmosphere being unsuitable for spacecraft to pass through: it is thick enough to cause some to break up and thin enough to fail at slowing down others safely. This means that with every launch, the spacecraft has a greater than fifty-percent chance of becoming a pile of Martian trash.

[1] **spacecraft** *n.* a vehicle used to travel in and explore space
[2] **crater** *n.* a round hole in the ground

So why do governments take the risk? Well, many argue that these missions fulfill humanity's need to "reach new **horizons**[3]," but that notion is rather abstract. More practically, missions increase national **prestige**[4] and benefit economies. The US is not alone in its interest in Mars: Russia landed two rovers on the planet in 1971 (though neither managed to transmit useful data), and India placed a spacecraft into orbit around it in 2014. In May of 2021, the *Zhurong* vehicle made China the third country to land a Mars rover successfully. Although competition between nations is peaceful for the moment, growing influence on the planet could lead to future military confrontations.

National space agencies are not the only ones invested in Mars exploration. Business leaders such as Elon Musk and Jeff Bezos agree on the benefits of humans traveling to Mars to set up colonies. The advantages they point to include easing overcrowding on Earth and allowing our planet to recover from environmental damage. In addition, businesses like Musk's Tesla could acquire valuable minerals from Mars, such as iron, titanium, nickel, and aluminum—material supplies that may soon become inadequate on Earth.

But making Mars **habitable**[5] enough to mine is extremely difficult and will require companies to provide water, food, oxygen, and heat to colonists millions of kilometers away. Although water would be relatively easy to find at the planet's ice caps and in underground lakes, energy is another matter. Large amounts of it would be needed to access water, grow food, provide heat, and fuel other human activity. As Mars is further from the sun than Earth and has regular dust storms, solar energy is not available, and the planet's thin atmosphere rules out wind power. Thus, the only realistic choice is nuclear power, which would require transporting nuclear fuel and a **reactor**[6] from Earth to Mars.

The planet also has high levels of **radiation**[7], which leads to cancer if not contained. So buildings on Mars would need to resist constant radiation and unpredictable events such as **solar flares**[8], effectively forcing settlers to live underground. Disasters are almost inevitable, and if private companies begin losing money, there is no guarantee they will remain involved. Therefore, governments may end up being forced to rescue their citizens, and with journey times at around seven months, any response would likely be too slow.

Even if we can successfully colonize Mars, this does not mean that we should. Exploring the planet has yielded little reward so far. Making the planet habitable could be damaging, expensive, and dangerous. Given all this, perhaps it would be best to admire the red planet through our telescopes and let its mysteries remain.

[3] **horizon** *n.* the limit of people's knowledge, ideas, and imagination
[4] **prestige** *n.* respect that is given to someone or something for its reputation, success, or influence
[5] **habitable** *adj.* suitable or possible to be lived in or on
[6] **reactor** *n.* a large machine in which atoms are divided or joined to produce energy
[7] **radiation** *n.* a form of energy emitted in the form of waves or particles that is dangerous to one's health
[8] **solar flare** *n.* a sudden explosion of energy on the sun which sends out high levels of heat and radiation

COMPREHENSION CHECK-UPS

1. Read paragraph 1. What can be inferred about the author's opinion of colonizing Mars?

____

____

2. According to paragraph 2, what did the *Viking* missions cause NASA to do?
   a. Start to look elsewhere in the solar system
   b. Change to a different type of spacecraft
   c. Decide to continue exploring Mars
   d. Reduce spending on Mars missions

3. According to paragraph 3, all of the following are true EXCEPT _______.
   a. spacecraft struggle to reduce speed when they reach Mars
   b. NASA's Perseverance mission was one of the twenty-eight failures
   c. many spacecraft are destroyed before they touch the surface of Mars
   d. four out of forty-nine missions to Mars were partly successful

4. According to paragraph 4, which is NOT a reason for governments to travel to Mars?
   a. To expand and stretch what humans think is possible
   b. To appear successful and important on the global stage
   c. To keep up with other nations around the world
   d. To recover crashed rovers and other spacecraft

5. According to paragraph 5, how could certain companies benefit from colonizing Mars?
   a. By allowing the Earth to mend itself
   b. By giving humanity more space to live
   c. By mining the planet's natural resources
   d. By getting government funding

6. According to paragraph 6, which of the following is true about colonizing Mars?

a. We would need energy to allow humans to drink water.

b. Wind energy cannot work because it is too cold.

c. Colonists could use the power created by dust storms.

d. Solar energy cannot work because the air is too thin.

7. Read paragraph 6. What can be inferred about the effect of dust storms on Mars?

____

____

8. What can be inferred from paragraph 6?

a. Mars has no natural sources of water.

b. Mars is incredibly dangerous to human life.

c. Mars has very stable weather conditions.

d. Mars is incredibly hot because of its thin atmosphere.

9. Which statement best restates the sentence, "Disasters are almost inevitable, and if private companies begin losing money, there is no guarantee they will remain involved." from paragraph 7?

a. Businesses could colonize Mars but are worried about accidents.

b. Businesses won't get involved in preventing disasters on Mars.

c. Businesses could pull out if expensive accidents occur on Mars.

d. Businesses might find that colonizing Mars is too difficult.

10. In paragraph 7, why does the author use the word "effectively"?

a. To show that colonists would not be able to work easily in the dark

b. To emphasize that colonizers would essentially be trapped underground

c. To explain that colonists would prefer to live above ground

d. To suggest that colonists would not be safe from radiation

MAPPING IDEAS

Use the word box to complete the graphic organizer. Then choose the best inference based on the statements.

WORD BOX		
realistic easy difficult regular require		
STATEMENTS		
1	**2**	**3**
But making Mars habitable enough to mine is extremely **1.** __________ and will **2.** __________ companies to provide water, food, oxygen, and heat to colonists millions of kilometers away.	Although water would be relatively **3.** __________ to find at the planet's ice caps and in underground lakes, energy is another matter.	As Mars is further from the sun than Earth and has **4.** __________ dust storms, solar energy is not available, and the planet's thin atmosphere rules out wind power. Thus, the only **5.** __________ choice is nuclear power, . . .
INFERENCES		

a. Those who live on Mars are likely to be unhealthy and will suffer from depression.
b. The risks of mining on Mars are outweighed by the potential profits companies could make.
c. The complications of sustaining human life could make colonizing Mars difficult.
d. The sustainable energies we use on Earth are likely to be adapted for use on Mars.

VOCABULARY REVIEW

Fill in the blanks with the correct words from the box. Change the form if needed.

classic	**investigate**	**allocate**	**abstract**
military	**acquire**	**inadequate**	**prestige**

1. The biggest classroom has been __________ to the new teacher because she has forty students per class.
2. The offer of $100 is completely __________ since the manufacturing cost alone is $110.
3. The greater the __________ of your university, the more you will impress employers.
4. This channel shows mainly __________ movies, so many of them are in black-and-white.
5. Over the last twenty years, I have managed to __________ many rare and unusual books.
6. Happiness is a(n) __________ concept that means something different to everyone.
7. Detectives are now __________ three people in connection with the crime.
8. The government has spent $250 million on guns and other __________ equipment.

CRITICAL-THINKING SKILL

Distinguishing Overgeneralizations

An overgeneralization is an overly broad statement that can be misleading and unfair. To avoid this, writers often use qualifying expressions. These include *most, some, a few, several, usually, often, probably, likely, and may/might*, among others.

Read the excerpts. Underline the words the writer uses to avoid overgeneralizations. Then summarize the excerpts.

1 Disasters are almost inevitable, and if private companies begin losing money, there is no guarantee they will remain involved. Therefore, governments may end up being forced to rescue their citizens, and with journey times at around seven months, any response would likely be too slow.

SUMMARIZE Write a short summary of the excerpt.

____

____

2 Even if we can successfully colonize Mars, this does not mean that we should. Exploring the planet has yielded little reward so far. Making the planet habitable could be damaging, expensive, and dangerous. Given all this, perhaps it would be best to admire the red planet through our telescopes and let its mysteries remain.

SUMMARIZE Write a short summary of the excerpt.

____

____

IDEAS IN DISCUSSION

1. Do you think it is likely that people will live on Mars in your lifetime? Why or why not?

2. What do you think could be gained from people living on Mars?

3. If you were offered a home and a job on Mars, would you go? Why or why not?

4. What might be some of the potential risks or challenges of establishing colonies on other planets?

5. Why do you think the US government allocates enormous amounts of money to space exploration? Is it driven by curiosity, profit, survival, or something else?

IDEAS IN WRITING

1. Write a paragraph comparing the exploration of Mars with the colonization of Mars. Should we do one, both, or neither?

2. Do you think your country should invest more in space exploration to prepare for the future? Write about your opinion and support it with specific reasons and details.

3. If space colonies are needed because of environmental damage on Earth, what actions should humans take to protect and restore our planet instead of colonizing others?

4. Write three reasons you would like to live on Mars within 250-300 words.

5. Write three reasons you would not want to live on Mars within 250-300 words.

ENGINEERING & IT

UNIT 4-1

Where Are Our Autonomous Cars?

Scan and find the tracks.

READING 1

SKILLS

Reading Skill:
Comparing and Contrasting

Critical-Thinking Skill:
Detecting the Author's Purpose

WARM-UP QUESTIONS

1. What do you think everyday life will be like one hundred years from now?
2. What sorts of things do you imagine when you think of science fiction?
3. In what part of your daily life do you rely on your smart devices?
4. What do you think is the number one cause of car accidents?
5. When you buy your own car, would you prefer an autonomous car (driverless car)?

BEFORE YOU READ

Read the statements. Check (✓) whether you agree or disagree with each statement. Discuss your answers with a partner.

	Strongly disagree	Disagree somewhat	Agree somewhat	Strongly agree
1. I enjoy driving.				
2. I think traffic laws in my country are good.				
3. I think traffic in my country is terrible.				
4. I think autonomous cars will change the world in my lifetime.				
5. I think autonomous cars will be safer than cars driven by people.				

VOCABULARY PREVIEW

1 Read the sentences. Circle the words closest in meaning to the words in bold.

1. Autonomous cars have been a popular **theme** for futurists to discuss.
   a. aspect　　b. incident　　c. concept

2. Science has tried hard to make this **vision** a reality, but it has still not been realized.
   a. foresight　　b. fantasy　　c. curiosity

3. Self-driving cars have been hypothesized to reduce serious traffic congestion by **approximately** seventy-five percent.
   a. roughly　　b. principally　　c. supposedly

4. When human error is taken out of the traffic **equation**, accident-related deaths and injuries will drop.
   a. calculation　　b. spectrum　　c. limelight

5. Many lives will be saved, **theoretically**, when human error is removed from driving.
   a. subsequently　　b. consistently　　c. hypothetically

6. The ride-hailing company Uber **suspended** its testing of driverless cars after a fatal accident.
   a. regulated　　b. ceased　　c. disbanded

7. A pedestrian death caused by a driverless car **highlights** the flaws in autonomous vehicle technology.
   a. emphasizes　　b. visualizes　　c. supplements

8. The service is **confined** to a single state during the testing period.
   a. restructured　　b. reduced　　c. restricted

2 Match the words in bold in section 1 above to their definitions below.

________ : close to a particular number or time although not exactly that number or time

________ : to limit an activity, person, or problem in some way

________ : a complex of variable factors that can only be understood if all the different influences are considered

________ : to throw a strong light on

________ : to cause to stop temporarily

________ : a subject or topic of discourse

________ : used to say what is possible, although it may not actually happen

________ : something that you imagine; a picture that you see in your mind

WHERE ARE OUR AUTONOMOUS CARS?

Track 07

1. **Reading Skill: Comparing and Contrasting**
   Comparing and contrasting are ways to describe how people, ideas, or things are similar or different. Sometimes writers use this to help define things or ideas.

2. **Critical-Thinking Skill: Detecting the Author's Purpose**
   Authors use specific information, arguments, and examples with clear language and explicit purposes to better convey their message. These include explaining/clarifying, emphasizing, arguing, persuading, and comparing and contrasting.

Most adult drivers would willingly acknowledge that driving, while usually the most convenient way to get around every day, can be an incredibly frustrating experience. This common human experience could be why cars that can operate **autonomously**[1] through artificial intelligence have been a common theme for **futurists'**[2] discussions for decades. Although science has made great strides in the past decade, some of us are getting impatient about realizing this vision: "It's 2020: Where are our self-driving cars?" asks a headline at the website *Vox*. It turns out that while autonomous vehicles are an attractive technology that has made great advances, perfecting them is much harder than we'd ever expected.

First, let's address the advantages of having a fully autonomous car: how many poor drivers have ever cried out in frustration after their third attempt at **parallel parking**[3]? The technology for a self-parking car has existed for a while. At the 2013 International Consumer Electronics Show, the Audi RS7 Sportback SUV gave an impressive performance, parking itself neatly into a spot while the driver stood on the curb and gave the vehicle commands from a smartphone app. No scratches, no bumps, and no need to leave an awkward note on someone's windshield.

Moreover, no one wants to sit aimlessly in their car every morning and afternoon while moving slowly along a congested highway with thousands of other irritable commuters. If there is even one

[1] **autonomously** *adv.* separately; independently
[2] **futurist** *n.* a person who tries to predict what the future will be like
[3] **parallel park** *v.* to park a vehicle so that its long side is parallel to the side of the road

fender-bender[4] along your route to work, you can be delayed up to an hour. A study by the US National Highway Traffic Safety Administration found that self-driving cars could reduce traffic jams by approximately seventy-five percent. The computers driving the cars will be able to communicate and basically **choreograph**[5] their own dance, in which commuters can safely move around one another at an even pace and without having to slow down to a crawl. The technology would allow cars to check in with each other, anticipate one another's movements, and calculate the best actions to perform.

Computers just do some things better than people do—and more importantly, they can perform several tasks at once. They aren't distracted by phones, passengers, or loud motorcycles, and they can't drink, take drugs, or get tired. Ninety percent of all car accidents are caused by the drivers' own mistakes. It's been estimated that once ninety percent of the cars on American roads are self-driving, 4.2 billion accidents could be avoided, and 21,700 lives saved annually. When human error is taken out of the equation, traffic accidents—and consequently, deaths and injuries—will **plummet**[6], at least theoretically.

But the key word is "theoretically." In recent years, engineers working on driverless cars have been forced to admit that the technical difficulties are greater than they had anticipated. The first death ever attributed to an autonomous vehicle occurred in 2018, when a **prototype**[7] car being tested by the ride-hailing company Uber and its human "safety driver" struck a woman walking her bicycle across the street. Unfortunately, the driver took his eyes off the road, and the car's autonomous mode failed to detect the woman in time to avoid a collision. An investigation found that the driver was **negligent**[8] and that the car's AI system had failed to indicate to the driver that a person was in its path. After the accident, Uber suspended its testing of driverless cars and later sold that division to another company.

The tragedy highlighted the fact that autonomous cars likely have a ways to go before the general population can trust that they'll be safe using them. It also raised questions about who bears responsibility for any harm done by self-driving vehicles—a question that has led many companies to re-evaluate their investment in this technology.

However, the effort continues. The recognized leader in the field is Waymo, a company formerly owned by Google and now by Google's parent company, Alphabet. Waymo has been working with several manufacturers to make commercially practical driverless cars. It has already launched the first fully public, fully autonomous taxi service—safely, so far—though, for now, it is confined to one city in the state of Arizona. In the meantime, for most of us, autonomous vehicles remain in the **realm**[9] of science fiction.

4	**fender-bender**	*n.*	a minor car accident
5	**choreograph**	*v.*	to design or arrange the movements of a dance
6	**plummet**	*v.*	to decrease suddenly
7	**prototype**	*n.*	an original or first model of something from which other forms are copied or developed
8	**negligent**	*adj.*	failing to take proper or normal care of something or someone
9	**realm**	*n.*	an area of interest, activity, or knowledge

COMPREHENSION CHECK-UPS

1. Which statement best restates the sentence, "Most adult drivers would willingly acknowledge that driving, while usually the most convenient way to get around every day, can be an incredibly frustrating experience." from paragraph 1?

a. People can agree that driving is both convenient and often frustrating.
b. Driving is the most convenient way to get around, even with its downsides.
c. The majority of adults get around every day by driving because it is easiest.
d. Most people who drive every day will confirm that it is a frustrating experience.

2. Read paragraph 1. Why does the author quote a headline from *Vox*?

____

____

3. According to paragraph 2, what did the first autonomous car do?

a. It sent a message to the driver's smartphone.
b. It drove around an electronics show floor.
c. It parked successfully at an electronics show.
d. It left a note for another driver.

4. In paragraph 3, which is NOT mentioned as an advantage of self-driving cars?

a. They would make fender-benders less costly.
b. They could reduce people's travel time to work.
c. They would be able to communicate with one another.
d. They could predict other cars' movements and respond.

5. In paragraph 3, why does the author use the word "crawl"?

a. To emphasize the simplicity of driving to and from a place
b. To suggest that people should move slowly to avoid an accident
c. To stress how slowly autonomous cars will move in the future
d. To emphasize how regular driving can be difficult

6. **Which of the following is NOT stated in paragraph 4?**

a. Self-driving cars' performance is not affected by passengers.
b. Drunk drivers cause the majority of car accidents in the US.
c. Autonomous cars could theoretically prevent billions of crashes per year.
d. Thousands of lives might be saved annually if most cars were autonomous.

7. **According to paragraph 5, what caused the first fatal accident involving a self-driving car?**

a. The car's computer system ceased to function.
b. The person in the car was not properly trained.
c. The woman's bicycle caused an error in the car's system.
d. The driver and the car's system failed to react in time.

8. **Read paragraph 6. What effect did the Uber accident have on other companies' thinking?**

____

____

9. **According to paragraph 7, which of the following is true about Waymo?**

a. It has a contract with Google to design autonomous cars.
b. It has not yet experienced any serious accidents.
c. It manufactures its self-driving cars in its own factories.
d. It has launched its service throughout one US state.

10. **What can be inferred from paragraph 7?**

a. Most companies want autonomous vehicles to remain science fiction.
b. Some companies still see potential in the technology despite the risks.
c. Google will provide a completely free public taxi service for Arizona.
d. Arizona is hoping to make all taxis in the state fully autonomous.

MAPPING IDEAS

Read the excerpts and fill in the blanks to describe the items discussed and the author's comparisons. Answers will vary.

	SIMILARITIES	DIFFERENCES
A study by the US National Highway Traffic Safety Administration found that self-driving cars could reduce traffic jams by approximately seventy-five percent. The computers driving the cars will be able to communicate and basically choreograph their own dance, in which commuters can safely move around one another at an even pace without having to slow down to a crawl.		Autonomous-driving cars are better for reducing traffic than regular cars because they can **1.** ___________.
It's been estimated that once ninety percent of the cars on American roads are self-driving, 4.2 billion accidents could be avoided, and 21,700 lives saved annually. When human error is taken out of the equation, traffic accidents—and consequently, deaths and injuries—will plummet, at least theoretically.		Autonomous-driving cars are better than human-driven cars because they won't be affected by **2.** ___________ which will result in fewer **3.** ___________.

VOCABULARY REVIEW

Fill in the blanks with the correct words from the box. Change the form if needed.

realm	**confine**	**theoretically**	**suspend**
equation	**highlight**	**plummet**	**approximately**

1. Sales of the new product ___________ after the competitor's new product came out.
2. We have ___________ thirty minutes until we present; that's enough time to redo this slide.
3. It is ___________ impossible for anything to travel faster than the speed of light.
4. The man was ___________ to his room after being diagnosed with a contagious disease.
5. Due to the flooding, all train services are ___________ until they can operate safely.
6. The latest break-in ___________ significant flaws in the company's security system.
7. In the ___________ of mathematics and physics, Sir Isaac Newton is highly regarded.
8. When considering a new job, you should consider the length of the commute as part of the ___________.

CRITICAL-THINKING SKILL

Detecting the Author's Purpose

Authors use specific information, arguments, and examples with clear language and explicit purposes to better convey their message. These include explaining/clarifying, emphasizing, arguing, persuading, comparing, and contrasting.

Read the excerpts. Evaluate them with a partner and answer the questions.

1

First, let's address the advantages of having a fully autonomous car: how many poor drivers have ever cried out in frustration after their third attempt at parallel parking? The technology for a self-parking car has existed for a while. At the 2013 International Consumer Electronics Show, the Audi RS7 Sportback SUV gave an impressive performance, parking itself neatly into a spot while the driver stood on the curb and gave the vehicle commands from a smartphone app.

PURPOSE Why does the author use the phrase "But the key word is 'theoretically'"?

____

SUMMARIZE Write a short summary of the author's purpose.

____

2

When human error is taken out of the equation, traffic accidents—and consequently, deaths and injuries—will plummet, at least theoretically.

But the key word is "theoretically." In recent years, engineers working on driverless cars have been forced to admit that the technical difficulties are greater than they had anticipated. The first death ever attributed to an autonomous vehicle occurred in 2018, when a prototype car being tested by the ride-hailing company Uber and its human "safety driver" struck a woman walking her bicycle across the street.

PURPOSE Why does the author use the phrase "But the key word is 'theoretically'"?

____

SUMMARIZE Write a short summary of the author's purpose.

____

IDEAS IN DISCUSSION

1. Why are some people hesitant to embrace autonomous vehicles?

2. Do you think the majority of cars will be autonomous one day? Why or why not?

3. Can you think of any other problems that autonomous vehicles might cause?

4. In the case of an accident involving a self-driving car, who should take the greatest responsibility: the car manufacturer, the software developer, or the person in the vehicle? Why?

5. When the majority of cars are autonomous, do you think we will still need a driver's license? Why or why not?

IDEAS IN WRITING

1. Write a paragraph about how life will be different if autonomous cars become the norm.

2. Summarize the upsides and downsides of self-driving cars that you learned from the reading and add your own ideas for both.

3. Imagine a future where autonomous devices—such as cars, robots, and other automated technologies—are a normal part of everyday life. In such a world, what responsibilities do you think humans should still hold? Support your answer with examples and reasoning.

4. Give examples of autonomous technology that have reduced our labor and daily tasks. Do you think this provides us with more spare time? How might it impact individual productivity and well-being?

5. The article describes a world where autonomous vehicles communicate with each other to reduce traffic. How do you think this type of technology could impact humans? Discuss both the positive and negative effects.

ENGINEERING & IT

UNIT 4-2 How Do You Like Me Now?

Scan and find the tracks.

READING 2

SKILLS

Reading Skill:
Extracting and Recalling Information

Critical-Thinking Skill:
Identifying Assumptions

WARM-UP QUESTIONS

1. How often do you use social media? Which sites do you use?

2. Are you happy and comfortable with the amount of time you spend on social media?

3. Could you survive a weekend without social media? What would you do with all that extra time?

4. Do you feel pressure to post or share certain things on social media? Why or why not?

5. Have you ever felt anxious or uneasy about missing out on something because of what you saw online?

BEFORE YOU READ

Read the statements. Check (✓) whether you agree or disagree with each statement. Discuss your answers with a partner.

	Strongly disagree	Disagree somewhat	Agree somewhat	Strongly agree
1. Social-media use leads to depression.				
2. Social media can be entertaining.				
3. Getting "likes" on social media makes me feel like a better person.				
4. There's a lot of bullying on social media.				
5. Social-media companies should prevent users from abusing their services.				

VOCABULARY PREVIEW

1 Read the sentences. Circle the words closest in meaning to the words in bold.

1. A small but significant number of US citizens meet the **criteria** for social-media addiction.
   a. definition b. amount c. transmission

2. Research has shown that young people are increasingly **depressed**.
   a. angry b. dismissive c. unhappy

3. Depression is more frequent in Gen Z than in **preceding** generations.
   a. later b. earlier c. larger

4. Those addicted to social media often **exhibit** poor self-control.
   a. contrast b. appear c. display

5. Social-media addicts often have trouble **concentrating**.
   a. focusing b. interpreting c. believing

6. Addicts find that they are **reliant** on social media to deal with negative emotions.
   a. reliable b. dependent c. respectful

7. Those who seek **validation** through social media sometimes have a poor self-image.
   a. friendship b. approval c. payment

8. The social **phenomenon** of increased youth suicide has been linked to social-media use.
   a. illusion b. idea c. issue

2 Match the words in bold in section 1 above to their definitions below.

________ : to direct one's attention or efforts towards a particular activity

________ : conditions or facts used as a standard by which something can be judged or defined

________ : unhappy and without hope

________ : to show or display something outwardly for others to see

________ : a fact or situation that exists or happens, especially one whose cause or explanation is in question

________ : existing or happening before someone or something

________ : needing a particular thing or person in order to continue or succeed

________ : the feeling that other people approve of and accept you, or something that gives you this feeling

HOW DO YOU LIKE ME NOW?

Track 08

1. **Reading Skill: Extracting and Recalling Information**
   Readers can recall important information by skimming the text. Search for keywords, phrases, dates, or numbers to find information quickly.

2. **Critical-Thinking Skill: Identifying Assumptions**
   Assumptions are often based on facts, ideas, or beliefs that are implied. It's important to evaluate if an assumption is reasonable or not.

Social media cannot be avoided in this day and age, and most people use it without a problem. However, some become addicted to it. Studies have estimated that between five and ten percent of Americans meet the criteria of social-media addiction. Like other behavioral addictions, social-media addiction causes physical and psychological harm, such as **withdrawal**[1] and mental **disorders**[2]. These illnesses are particularly dangerous and common among children and young adults. Reports on the mental health of Generation Z, or Gen Z (people born between the late 1990s and early 2010s), have shown that teenagers are more stressed and depressed than preceding generations. Thus, researchers are working to understand social-media addiction, its causes, and its effects to find ways to address it.

To identify social-media addiction, scientists have found some common symptoms that addicts share. For example, addicts often exhibit poor decision-making and self-control. They frequently ignore real-life relationships, fail to maintain work or school responsibilities, and lose interest in maintaining their health. Additionally, addicts are likely to have **mood swings**[3] and difficulty concentrating.

The causes of social-media addiction are complex and differ from person to person. However,

1 **withdrawal** *n.* the unpleasant physical and mental effects that result when you stop doing or taking something (such as a drug) that has become a habit

2 **disorder** *n.* an illness or condition that interferes with normal physical or mental functions

3 **mood swing** *n.* a sudden change in mood that is hard to explain

most researchers compare it to gambling because of the way it affects the reward areas of users' brains. They found that when people receive a like, retweet, share, etc., on social media, they get a **rush**[4] that is similar to the feeling that gamblers get when they win. This rush is created by a **neurotransmitter**[5] called dopamine, which helps create feelings of pleasure and motivation. For most users, this rush is enjoyable but not addictive. However, addicts will **pursue**[6] this rush even at the cost of their health. Social-media addicts can also become reliant on the activity not only for recreational purposes but also as a way to cope with stress, loneliness, and depression. This can lead to further problems. For example, people who look for validation or praise online might develop disorders linked to their self-image, such as body dysmorphia—a mental health condition in which the subject spends a lot of time worrying about their appearance.

The consequences of years of social-media addiction are growing increasingly apparent. A study by the JAMA Network of medical journals found that America's youth suicide rates reached a high in 2017. Most theories that try to explain this phenomenon find that social-media use can be linked to mental health issues. As noted earlier, reports on the mental health of Gen Z show that they're growing increasingly stressed and depressed. Many experts believe that **stressors**[7] found on social media significantly contribute to youth depression. Some of these stressors include economic problems, fear of not fitting in, fear of school shootings, and worries over the high cost of college. Another common stressor is bullying, particularly **cyberbullying**[8]. According to the American Psychological Association, thirty-five percent of Gen Zers list it as a stressor.

In terms of addressing social-media addiction, the most common advice is to limit screen time. However, this is easier said than done. Technology doesn't compare with other bad habits like gambling since technology is an essential part of everyday life. We use devices at school and work for entertainment, communication, and more. Since teenagers and their parents have trouble breaking the addiction cycle and restricting screen time, perhaps social-media companies should work to reduce their psychological impact. In fact, some companies are taking this idea seriously. For example, Instagram, the popular photo and video-sharing app, made its viewable "like" count optional.

Social media is a powerful tool that's been allowed to exist relatively untouched by outside regulation. However, growing concern over its effects on youth has led parents and health experts to the breaking point. For Generation Z, the damage might have already been done. But this problem must be solved if we hope to protect the mental health of future generations.

4	**rush**	*n.*	(*informal*) a sudden thrill; an intense feeling of excitement
5	**neurotransmitter**	*n.*	a chemical that carries messages between parts of the brain called neurons
6	**pursue**	*v.*	to try to gain; to seek
7	**stressor**	*n.*	something that causes great worry or emotional difficulty
8	**cyberbullying**	*n.*	the activity of using the internet to harm or frighten another person

COMPREHENSION CHECK-UPS

1. Which of the following is stated in paragraph 1?

   a. At least one in five Americans has some form of social-media addiction.
   b. Mental disorders are more common and dangerous among the young.
   c. Most of Generation Z reached adulthood in the early 2010s.
   d. Teenagers of all generations experience equal amounts of depression.

2. According to paragraph 2, all of the following are true about social-media addicts EXCEPT ________.

   a. they find it easy to get a job on social media
   b. they struggle to maintain offline friendships
   c. they may lose focus on staying fit and healthy
   d. they may have unpredictable emotions

3. Which of the following is NOT stated in paragraph 3?

   a. When social-media users notice a "like," a chemical is released in their brains.
   b. Research has shown that gambling addicts are likely to become addicted to social media.
   c. Seeking praise through social media can lead to mental illnesses like body dysmorphia.
   d. Users can come to need social media as a way to cover up feelings of sadness and isolation.

4. Read paragraph 3 and write a definition of *dopamine*.

   ____

   ____

5. What can be inferred about body dysmorphia from paragraph 3?

   a. It is a very rare problem.
   b. It makes people less attractive.
   c. It mainly affects social-media addicts.
   d. It can cause mental and physical harm.

6. **Which of the following is true according to paragraph 4?**

a. High-school shootings and economic worries reached a record high in 2017.

b. The majority of Gen Zers named social media as a major cause of stress.

c. The JAMA Network is calling for social-media companies to reduce addiction.

d. Research has shown that Gen Zers are suffering from high levels of depression.

7. **According to paragraph 5, what is true of Instagram?**

a. It has changed one feature of the site to make it easier to use.

b. It is helping parents track their children's online activities.

c. It changed its service to help lessen the harm caused by social media.

d. It believes the changes it has made will increase its popularity.

8. **Which statement best restates the sentence, "Since teenagers and their parents have trouble breaking the addiction cycle and restricting screen time, perhaps social-media companies should work to reduce their psychological impact." from paragraph 5?**

a. Since addiction is common, teenagers ought to stay off social media.

b. Social-media companies should restrict young people from using their services.

c. Social-media companies should limit users' screen time to reduce negative psychological impacts on users.

d. Since social-media addiction is difficult to break, social-media companies should reduce the harm they cause.

9. **Read paragraph 5. Why does the author believe social media is so hard to avoid?**

____

____

10. **In paragraph 6, why does the author say, "the damage might have already been done"?**

a. To suggest that it may be too late to help Gen Z

b. To suggest that those born in the future may suffer more

c. To suggest that social-media companies may soon be punished

d. To suggest that future generations will not have access to social media

MAPPING IDEAS

Read the opening sentences from the reading and match them to the correct detail sentences below.

HOW DO YOU LIKE ME NOW?		
PARAGRAPH #	**OPENING SENTENCES**	**DETAILS**
Paragraph 1	Social media cannot be avoided in this day and age, and most people use it without a problem.	**1.** ________
Paragraph 2	To identify social-media addiction, scientists have found some common symptoms that addicts share.	**2.** ________
Paragraph 3	The causes of social-media addiction are complex and differ from person to person.	**3.** ________
Paragraph 4	The consequences of years of social-media addiction are growing increasingly apparent.	**4.** ________
Paragraph 5	In terms of addressing social-media addiction, the most common advice is to limit screen time.	**5.** ________
Paragraph 6	Social media is a powerful tool that's been allowed to exist relatively untouched by outside regulation.	**6.** ________

DETAILS

a. Earlier generations did not experience as much stress and depression as Gen Z.
b. It might be too late to reverse the harm done to Gen Z.
c. Different types of addiction involve dopamine—a brain chemical that causes a rush.
d. Some companies are looking for ways to solve the problem, such as not counting "likes."
e. There are many causes of stress, including not being able to afford higher education.
f. People with addictions may lose touch with their friends and fail to take good care of themselves.

VOCABULARY REVIEW

Fill in the blanks with the correct words from the box. Change the form if needed.

criteria	**precede**	**exhibit**	**concentrate**
reliant	**validation**	**pursue**	**disorder**

1. Many find that a quiet room without distractions is best for ______________ on reading.
2. A dermatologist is a physician who treats diseases and ______________ of the skin.
3. People who are genuinely confident and secure rarely require ______________ from others.
4. All job applicants must meet several ______________ in order to be considered for an interview.
5. If you're good at making arguments and persuading people, maybe you should think about ______________ a career in law.
6. Children who ______________ problematic behavior might benefit from a specialist's help.
7. The current president is against many of the laws supported by the ______________ president.
8. Since she broke her leg, Janice has been ______________ on family to bring her groceries.

CRITICAL-THINKING SKILL

Identifying Assumptions

Arguments often include assumptions—facts, ideas, or beliefs that are not directly stated but implied. Some assumptions are reasonable, while others are not. Not everything has to be proven. However, writers often jump to conclusions and use faulty or illogical assumptions to build arguments. For example:

(1) Soldiers are brave.

(2) Brave people are strong.

(3) Therefore, all strong people are soldiers.

Read the excerpts and conclusion sentences. Put a checkmark (✓) next to the valid conclusions and a cross (X) next to the conclusions with a faulty assumption.

1

Since teenagers and their parents have trouble breaking the addiction cycle and restricting screen time, perhaps social-media companies should work to reduce their psychological impact. In fact, some companies are taking this idea seriously. For example, Instagram, the popular photo and video-sharing app, made its viewable "like" count optional.

CONCLUSION SENTENCES

a. ______ Companies that won't do the same do not care about mental health.

b. ______ This change could reduce stress and lower the risk of addiction.

c. ______ Companies that promote mental health are more profitable than those that don't.

2

Many experts believe that stressors found on social media are significantly contributing to youth depression. Some of these stressors include economic problems, fear of not fitting in, fear of school shootings, and worries over the high cost of college. Another common stressor is bullying, particularly cyberbullying. According to the American Psychological Association, thirty-five percent of Gen Zers list it as a stressor.

CONCLUSION SENTENCES

a. ______ We have been able to identify new social problems thanks to social media.

b. ______ Gen Zers are more sensitive to bullying than preceding generations.

c. ______ Social media draws attention to real-world problems and can cause stress.

IDEAS IN DISCUSSION

1. In what ways does social media change people's behavior?
2. How would you change social media to make it a healthier environment?
3. Will you attempt to reduce your use of social media in the future? Why or why not?
4. How often do you feel like social media is distracting you from things you actually care about?
5. Do you feel like you're in control of your internet usage, or does it feel like it's controlling you?

IDEAS IN WRITING

1. Write a paragraph about how social media can negatively affect people's lives and what can be done to lessen its impact.
2. Write about how the pursuit of likes, shares, or follows influences your self-esteem or mood. Do you think you'd feel different about social media if those features didn't exist?
3. Reflect on the ways social media affects your daily routine. Have you noticed any habits that might indicate a dependency on social media?
4. Should social media companies be held responsible for the negative impacts of their platforms? What steps can they take to promote healthier social media use?
5. Discuss the potential benefits of social media, such as connecting with others, staying informed, and pursuing hobbies. How can we harness the positive aspects of social media while minimizing the negative impacts?

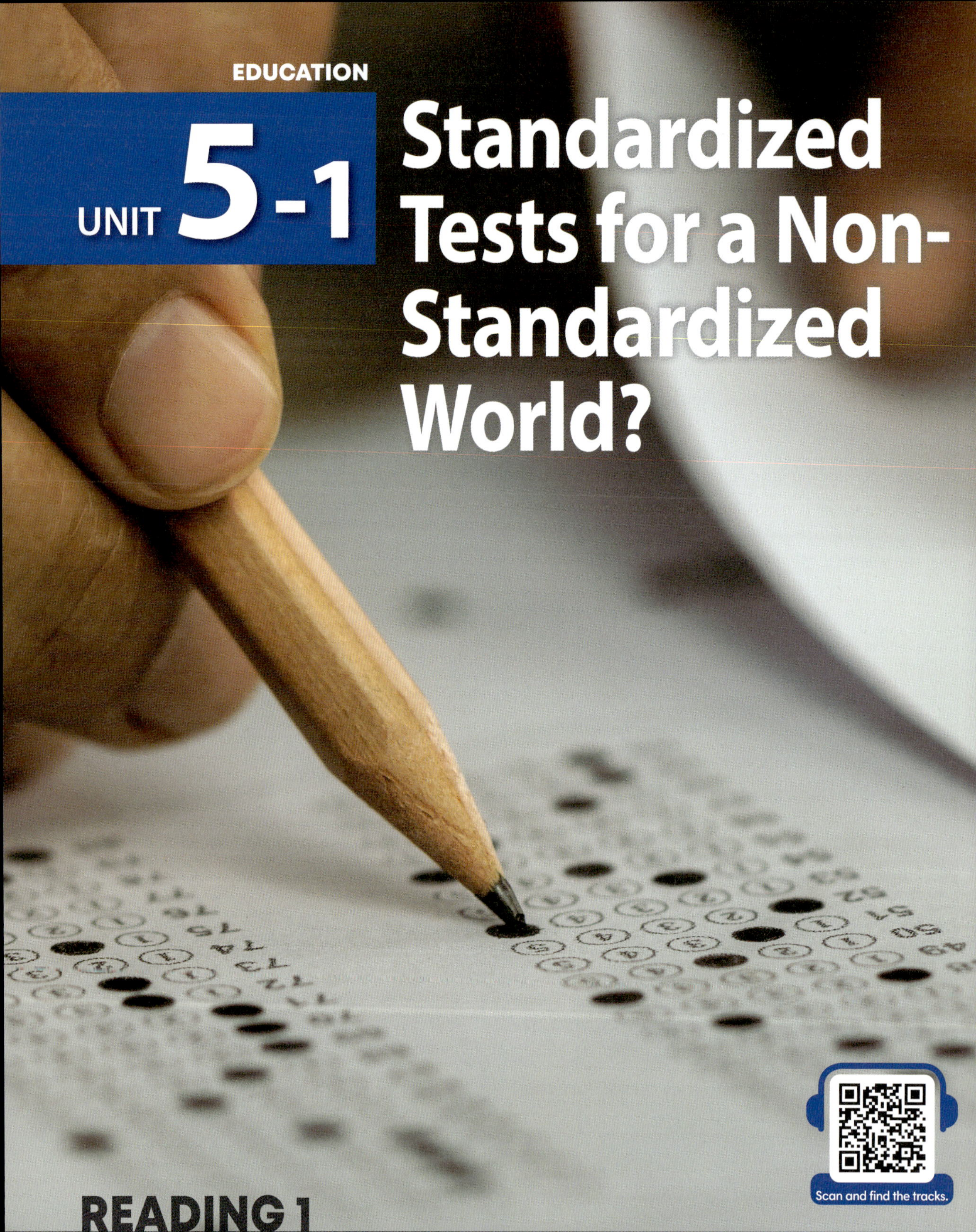

EDUCATION

UNIT 5-1 Standardized Tests for a Non-Standardized World?

Scan and find the tracks.

READING 1

SKILLS

Reading Skill:
Summarizing

Critical-Thinking Skill:
Identifying Premises and Conclusions

WARM-UP QUESTIONS

1. When was your last test or exam? When is your next one?

2. What are some ways to test a student's abilities?

3. What are some challenges students face during exams?

4. How can schools and parents help students manage test-related stress?

5. What are the pros and cons of standardized testing?

BEFORE YOU READ

Rank the different assignments that can be used to assess students' abilities from 1 (most comprehensive) to 5 (least comprehensive). Discuss your rankings with a partner.

__________ Presentations

__________ Multiple-choice tests

__________ Long-form written tests

__________ Essays

__________ Debates

VOCABULARY PREVIEW

1 Read the sentences. Circle the words closest in meaning to the words in bold.

1. Historically, students taking exams had to debate various **topics** with lecturers.
   a. parameters b. subjects c. points

2. The older examination format was unfair because it contained too many **variables**.
   a. elements b. controversies c. mechanisms

3. Over time, we have **amended** exams to make them fairer and more accurate.
   a. unified b. enhanced c. perfected

4. Students take **identical** tests in modern exams such as SATs.
   a. distinct b. miscellaneous c. indistinguishable

5. During the COVID-19 pandemic, students who were less fortunate **economically** found it hard to **replace** lost lessons.
   a. financially b. domestically c. intellectually

6. We can **ignore** the socio-economic issues, but the question remains: do exams really work?
   a. scorn b. mark c. overlook

7. One expert has suggested that tests are of most **benefit** to schools in revealing their rankings.
   a. assistance b recourse c. pleasure

8. It might be better if exams were just one **component** in a broader selection of assessments.
   a. detail b. summation c. factor

2 Match the words in bold in section 1 above to their definitions below.

________ : to change some of the words of a document or text

________ : something that produces good or helpful results or effects or that promotes well-being

________ : a constituent part; ingredient

________ : in a way that relates to money, income, or one's financial situation

________ : the same

________ : to refuse to take notice of

________ : a subject or theme that is discussed, written about, or studied

________ : a number, amount, or situation that can change

STANDARDIZED TESTS FOR A NON-STANDARDIZED WORLD?

Track 09

1. **Reading Skill: Summarizing**
   A summary restates the main points of a passage or work. Summarizing can help you focus and remember the most important information.

2. **Critical-Thinking Skill: Identifying Premises and Conclusions**
   An argument includes premises (reasons) and a conclusion. Reasons are sometimes indicated with expressions such as *because, since, thus, therefore,* etc.

As we might recognize them, the earliest form of exams took place at universities in the eleventh century. They were oral and involved small groups of **elite**[1] candidates who were expected to debate with lecturers on topics from philosophy to the natural sciences. It was a system **fraught**[2] with variables and **inequities**[3]. It wasn't until the nineteenth century that written exams became common. Since then, many would claim, we have gradually amended examinations to be fairer, more effective, and more relevant—but are the exams students take today really fit for purpose?

Today, exams such as the Scholastic Assessment Test (SATs)—which secure entry to universities—are nationally standardized. This standardization means that, unlike those early exams, all students take identical tests to make a "fair" comparison of many students. However, according to critics, tests such as the SAT inherently favor the wealthy. The COVID-19 pandemic exacerbated this issue. With schools closed, economically disadvantaged students were less likely to encounter crucial alternatives like individual **tutelage**[4] or homeschooling. Many also found that their tests were repeatedly rescheduled or canceled at the last minute; others could not take the exams at all. Such was the **prevalence**[5] of the problem that 1,600 US universities, including every Ivy League college, signed up to the "test-optional" movement. This meant that in 2021 at

1	**elite**	*n.*	the richest, most powerful, best educated, or best-trained group in a society
2	**fraught**	*adj.*	full of unpleasant things such as problems or dangers
3	**inequities**	*n.*	qualities of being unfair, or something that is not fair or equal
4	**tutelage**	*n.*	help, advice, or teaching about how to do something
5	**prevalence**	*n.*	the fact that something is very common or happens often

least, colleges would not necessarily take SAT scores into account when considering applications. Initially, the test-optional movement was an emergency response to the pandemic. Still, like many such measures, we may find that its flexibility makes it a fairer option in the future.

Even if we ignore the socio-economic issues behind standardized exams, the question remains: are they really an effective way to find out how much a student knows? Some students are emotionally and psychologically better suited than others to the pressure of providing evidence—on one given day—of several years of education. This fact was made clear when the situation surrounding the COVID-19 pandemic shone a **spotlight**[6] on the mental impact of tests. As schools closed and college application deadlines approached, stress among students skyrocketed. Many feared that the lost months would affect the rest of their lives. In the UK, a 2020 study by Rahim Hirji for Quizlet found that of 1,400 teenagers, eighty-five percent were stressed or anxious. In response, the UK and other governments instructed teachers to rely on their detailed first-hand knowledge of students' long-term performance to decide grades.

Even under normal conditions, some argue that the heavy reliance on examinations leads to ineffective education, **rote learning**[7], and "teaching to the test." Critics like Dr. Robin Harwick argue that current students are not given a **holistic**[8] education but are simply taught to score highly. "Standardized tests are only useful for measuring standardized minds," says Dr. Harwick. "However, humans are not standardized, nor do we want them to be." Another argument against standardized tests is that the prevalence of multiple-choice exams—which computers can quickly grade—pushes students to learn how to deduce logical answers rather than use independent critical thinking. In addition, schools seem to benefit most from teaching students to succeed at quantifiable tests since school ranking tables are now widely published and referred to by parents. Their **prominence**[9] leads schools and teachers to feel pressure to focus on test results, perhaps at the expense of other, less tangible aspects of educational development.

Of course, supporters of standardized tests would point to the transferable skills required in studying for them, including organization, preparation, and self-discipline. In fact, the very stress that some cite as a problem could also be seen as a useful experience. We will all one day be required to **retrieve**[10] and apply information under pressure in our adult lives. Thus, exams serve a clear purpose as one part of an educational strategy, and even critics wouldn't call for their total elimination. However, many would argue that too much weight is placed on them and that it would be fairer and less stressful to think of exams as just one component in a wider grading system of long-term coursework, which includes research, presentations, and essays.

[6] **spotlight** *n.* something that directs public attention to a particular issue
[7] **rote learning** *n.* learning something to be able to repeat it from memory rather than to understand it
[8] **holistic** *adj.* dealing with or treating the whole of something or someone and not just a part
[9] **prominence** *n.* the state of being easily seen or well known
[10] **retrieve** *v.* to find and bring back something

COMPREHENSION CHECK-UPS

1. According to paragraph 1, what was the problem with the earliest exams?

   a. They were difficult to pass.
   b. They were easy to cheat on.
   c. They only tested sciences.
   d. They had many inequities.

2. According to paragraph 2, how did colleges respond to the COVID-19 pandemic?

   a. They offered to pay for individual classes.
   b. They agreed to ignore students' SAT scores.
   c. They canceled SAT tests on short notice.
   d. They accepted fewer applications.

3. Read paragraph 2 and write the reason why many colleges signed up for the "test-optional" movement.

   ____

   ____

4. According to paragraph 3, all of the following are true EXCEPT _______.

   a. some students are better suited for the pressures of standardized tests
   b. UK teachers were instructed not to give students grades in 2020
   c. the pandemic further emphasized the negative impacts of testing
   d. studies found that the majority of UK teenagers were stressed

5. Which of the following is NOT stated in paragraph 4?

   a. "Teaching to the test" happens primarily in highly ranked schools.
   b. Standardized testing does not encourage independent critical thinking.
   c. Multiple-choice exams make checking test answers quicker.
   d. School rankings pressure some teachers to teach to the test.

6. In paragraph 4, why does Dr. Harwick say that "students are not standardized"?

a. To explain why exams are commonly used in academics
b. To suggest that exams are not appropriate for everyone
c. To explain that exam results will always be unpredictable
d. To suggest that exams succeed at standardizing knowledge

7. According to paragraph 5, how are exams useful?

a. They improve a student's ability to deal with stress.
b. They teach students to deduce information quickly.
c. They provide practice for the pressures of adult life.
d. They are fairer and less stressful than other test formats.

8. Which statement best restates the sentence, "Thus, exams serve a clear purpose as one part of an educational strategy, and even critics wouldn't call for their total elimination." from paragraph 5?

a. Exams are valuable, but even so, some would like to see them stopped.
b. Exams are useful, and many believe they are the most efficient way to learn.
c. Exams serve a clear purpose but only work well in certain educational strategies.
d. Exams are a beneficial tool, and few would want to eliminate them altogether.

9. Read paragraph 5 and write why stress caused by exams could be helpful.

____

____

10. What can be inferred from paragraph 5?

a. Presentations test different skills than those found in standardized tests.
b. Critics believe that exams should be removed from educational strategies.
c. Those who score well on exams are more likely to perform well at work.
d. Coursework and presentations are not as stressful as examinations.

MAPPING IDEAS

Read the statements that summarize the passage. Then put the answers in the correct order to complete the graphic organizer.

STANDARDIZED TESTS FOR A NON-STANDARDIZED WORLD				
PARAGRAPH 1	PARAGRAPH 2	PARAGRAPH 3	PARAGRAPH 4	PARAGRAPH 5
1. ________	2. ________	3. ________	4. ________	5. ________

STATEMENTS

a. Standardized exams can lead to poor educational practices and competition between schools.
b. Exams place a large amount of stress on students and therefore suit some more than others.
c. There are educational benefits to exams, but they should be used as part of a series of assessments.
d. Standardized tests may seem fair, but they may not be the best way to assess students' abilities.
e. The COVID-19 pandemic helped to show that only certain students can succeed if being evaluated solely by standardized tests.

VOCABULARY REVIEW

Fill in the blanks with the correct words from the box. Change the form if needed.

topic	variable	amend	identical
economically	benefit	prevalence	prominence

1. The ________________ of cycling include being both a low-impact and an excellent cardiovascular exercise.
2. The novelist Charles Dickens first came to ________________ by publishing in magazines.
3. The ________________ of cars in some cities leads to breathing problems among children.
4. After complaints about its content, the online article was ________________.
5. Contestants on the quiz show could choose questions from four ________________.
6. The speed of a boat depends on many ________________, including size, weight, shape, and weather conditions.
7. Many people in Nigeria are ________________ vulnerable, even though the country is rich in resources.
8. Aside from a bow and some eyelashes, Minnie and Mickey Mouse are nearly ________________.

CRITICAL-THINKING SKILL

Identifying Premises and Conclusions

Arguments include reasons called premises and a conclusion. Writers might sometimes state their conclusion before their premises. Identifying the premises and conclusion will help you better understand a writer's argument. For example:

People who care about their health should exercise daily (conclusion).

Research shows that people who exercise thirty minutes or more a day have less risk of developing heart disease and cancer (premise).

1 **Read the excerpts from the reading. Each contains an argument. For each part in the excerpt, circle P for premise or C for a conclusion.**

	STATEMENTS
1. (P / C)	However, according to Forbes, tests such as the SAT inherently favor the wealthy. In addition, the COVID-19 pandemic exacerbated this issue.
(P / C)	With schools closed, economically disadvantaged students were less likely to encounter crucial alternatives like individual tutelage or homeschooling.
(P / C)	Many also found that their tests were repeatedly rescheduled or canceled at the last minute; others could not take the exams at all.
2. (P / C)	Of course, supporters of standardized tests would point to the transferable skills required in studying for them, including organization, preparation, and self-discipline.
(P / C)	In fact, the very stress that some cite as a problem could also be seen as a useful experience. We will all one day be required to retrieve and apply information under pressure in our adult lives.
(P / C)	Thus, exams serve a clear purpose as one part of an educational strategy, and even critics wouldn't call for their total elimination.

IDEAS IN DISCUSSION

1. **What are some common methods used to evaluate student learning?** *Consider what role standardized tests play in today's education system.*
2. **How do standardized tests impact students' mental health and well-being?** *Think about the pressure to perform well, the fear of failure, and the potential for long-term negative effects.*
3. **How would you change exams to make them fairer or less stressful?** *Considering the*

historical context and current role of tests in education, explore how technology can impact our assessment of student performance.

4. **What are alternative methods of assessing student knowledge and skills? Would you like more of your grades to come from coursework such as essays, presentations, and debates?** *Consider the evolving needs of students and society, as well as the limitations of traditional testing methods.*
5. **How can we create a more holistic assessment system that measures a student's full potential?** *Think about alternative assessment methods, such as portfolios, projects, and performance-based assessments.*

IDEAS IN WRITING

1. **Criticize Standardized Tests:** Do standardized tests accurately measure a student's potential? Standardized tests, while intended to promote fairness and objectivity, often perpetuate systemic inequalities and fail to accurately measure a student's true potential. The excessive reliance on standardized tests in education can stifle creativity, critical thinking, and a love of learning, ultimately hindering students' long-term success.
2. **The Impact of Standardized Tests on Mental Health:** How do standardized tests contribute to student stress and anxiety? What are the long-term consequences of high-stakes testing on students' mental health? The high-stakes nature of standardized tests can lead to unethical practices, such as test preparation cramming and cheating, which undermine the purpose of assessment and create a culture of fear and anxiety.
3. **Alternative Assessment Methods:** What are the advantages and disadvantages of alternative assessment methods, such as portfolios, projects, and performance-based assessments? Can alternative assessments provide a more accurate measure of student learning and growth? A more holistic approach to assessment, incorporating a variety of methods such as portfolios, projects, and performance-based assessments, can provide a more accurate and equitable evaluation of student learning.
4. **The Role of Technology in Assessment:** How can technology be used to enhance the assessment process? What are the ethical implications of using AI and machine learning in education? The integration of technology into assessment can enhance the efficiency, accuracy, and personalization of the evaluation process. While technology offers numerous benefits, it is essential to use it responsibly and ethically to ensure that it does not exacerbate existing inequalities or compromise the integrity of the assessment process.
5. **The Future of Education:** What does the future hold for standardized tests? How can we create a more student-centered and personalized approach to education? What role should standardized tests play in a 21st-century education system? It is imperative to prioritize ethical considerations in the development, administration, and interpretation of standardized tests to ensure that they are used fairly and responsibly.

EDUCATION

UNIT **5-2**

The Benefits of a Creative Education

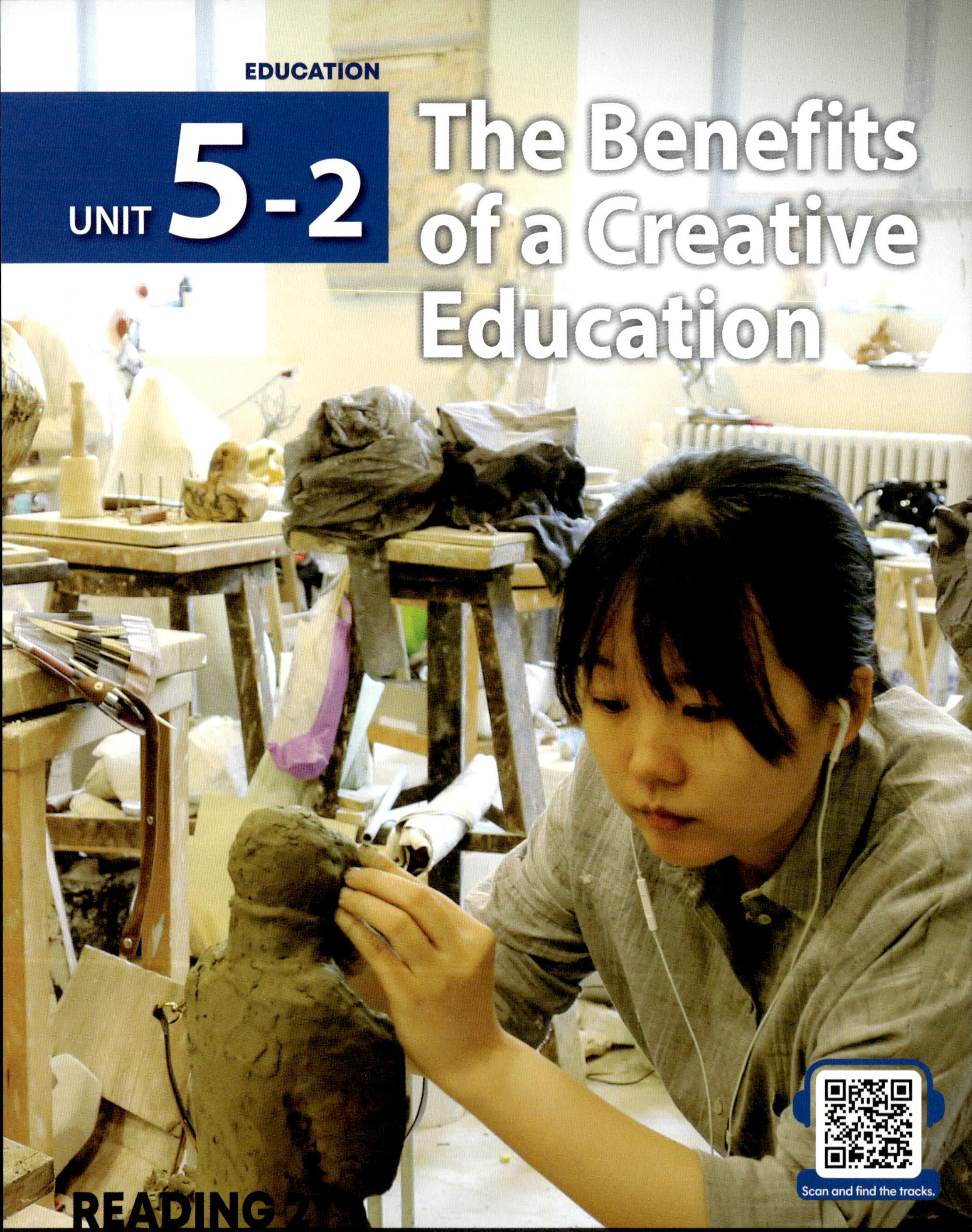

Scan and find the tracks.

READING 2

SKILLS

Reading Skill:
Identifying the Author's Point of View

Critical-Thinking Skill:
Finding Fallacies

WARM-UP QUESTIONS

1. Which school subjects require the most creativity?
2. Do you think it's possible to teach yourself to be more creative? Why or why not?
3. What are practical subjects and what are impractical subjects?
4. What kinds of art lessons have you taken? When did you take them?
5. What are the benefits of your experience learning art?

BEFORE YOU READ

Rank the statements from 1 (most agree with) to 6 (least agree with). Discuss your rankings with a partner.

_________ I enjoy music and/or art.

_________ I think math is more important than music.

_________ I want to work in a creative field.

_________ I think people who can play an instrument are usually smart.

_________ I wish we could study creative subjects more often in school.

_________ I think studying art and music in school is a waste of time.

VOCABULARY PREVIEW

1 Read the sentences. Circle the words closest in meaning to the words in bold.

1. Many Finnish people believe that creative activities are beneficial because they teach **cooperation**.
   a. charity b. teamwork c. assistance

2. In Finland, the education system benefits from the **availability** of funds.
   a. certainty b. manageability c. accessibility

3. Education is more heavily **oriented** toward creativity in some countries than others.
   a. aimed b. ranged c. assured

4. In the US and UK, schools that focus on creativity can be **prohibitively** expensive.
   a. restrictively b. notably c. productively

5. It can seem **illogical** to teach creative subjects to children in poorer areas.
   a. theatrical b. unreasonable c. inconsequential

6. Employers like creativity, a skill taught by letting children think outside of standard **parameters**.
   a. boundaries b. lessons c. expectations

7. The arts **contribute** to the wealth of nations.
   a. add b. withdraw c. permit

8. For example, the UK **culture** industry adds £11 billion to the country every year.
   a. design b. sciences c. arts

2 Match the words in bold in section 1 above to their definitions below.

________ : the extent to which something can be bought, used, reached, or found

________ : to give something, such as money, goods, or time to help a person, group, cause, or organization

________ : a situation in which people work together to do something

________ : music, art, theater, literature, etc.

________ : not reasonable, wise, or practical, usually because it is due to emotions rather than by careful thought

________ : directed towards or interested in something

________ : any of a set of physical properties whose values determine the characteristics or behavior of something

________ : in a way that stops something because it is too much; restrictive

THE BENEFITS OF A CREATIVE EDUCATION

Track 10

1. **Reading Skill: Identifying the Author's Point of View**
   A point of view is the attitude or position a person takes on a subject. A neutral point of view doesn't choose sides. A biased point of view is either influenced by outside forces or the writer's opinion.

2. **Critical-Thinking Skill: Finding Fallacies**
   A fallacy is faulty reasoning used to create an argument. There are many kinds of fallacies. Finding them will help you make strong objections.

The word "school" doesn't have to **evoke**[1] the feeling of being stuck at a desk solving math problems or memorizing the periodic table. Today, some countries and leading institutions are utilizing and thereby illustrating the educational benefits of creative activities, and these benefits range from academic to personal and social.

In Finland, there has long been a focus on learning through play; in fact, children do not begin school until they are six years old, giving them more time to develop and learn at home in a relaxed, informal setting. When they do arrive at school, their first "pre-primary" year is defined mainly by play, and it is not until age seven that a more formal academic curriculum is introduced. As their education continues, rigid, **didactic**[2] teaching and standardized tests are given far less significance than in many nations. Instead, there is a strong focus on art and music education: children must have at least two to four hours of music lessons each week, and, as secondary school begins, visual arts, crafts, media arts, music, literary art, circus art, dance, and theater are all taught regularly.

Besides **tangibly**[3] promoting creativity, cooperation, communication, and collaboration (the four Cs), creative activities are believed by many Finns to reinforce learning in other subject areas. There is evidence to support this notion. Finland frequently tops worldwide educational rankings, and it is perhaps no coincidence that the northern European nation also regularly ranks as the happiest in the world. Of course, it should also be remembered that Finland is a wealthy country

[1] **evoke** *v.* to bring to mind or recollection
[2] **didactic** *adj.* taught in a way that is one-sided, fixed, and unwilling to change
[3] **tangibly** *adv.* in a real way that you can touch, feel, see, experience, etc.

with a relatively small population. Its education system and comfortable way of life rely not only on creativity but also on the availability of investment in education. These investments come largely from the country's 56.95 percent income tax rate.

In other parts of the world, education is not as heavily oriented toward creativity. Although developed countries like the US and UK are home to private institutions such as Steiner Schools, which prioritize learning through play, these are often prohibitively expensive. In publicly funded schools, art, drama, and music departments are under pressure through a lack of funding. In fact, for each student at an ordinary school in the UK, the 2021 budget allowed just £9.40 ($12.79) for art and music education each year. Perhaps this could help explain why the number of students choosing to continue in art education after the age of fourteen—when it becomes **elective**[4]—has dropped by twenty percent over the last ten years.

Of course, it can seem illogical to fund abstract, "**impractical**[5]" subjects like painting or dance in less wealthy areas with high unemployment. But creative subjects have been proven to encourage children to remain in education and to achieve more. According to research, in schools with low participation in the arts, around twenty-two percent of low socio-economic status children do not graduate. Meanwhile, only four percent drop out in schools with high arts participation. And, of those who remain, students who take three to four years of arts and music education have been found to average 100 points better on SATs than those who do not. Furthermore, graduates' options improve from an education in the arts. When asked, seventy-seven percent of employers agreed on the number-one attribute they are looking for in new employees: creativity. This skill can only be developed by encouraging students to think independently and outside of **prescribed**[6] parameters.

The arts themselves can also contribute to nations financially. Today, the UK's culture industry adds around £11 billion to the economy. Of course, most students will not become professional musicians or film directors. Still, as the twentieth-century American painter Grant Wood put it: "The aim of art education in public schools is not to make more professional artists but to teach people to live happier, fuller lives." It can also build emotional intelligence and encourage empathy: leading universities such as Harvard and Columbia now include art lectures and **modules**[7] like painting in their medical schools' **curricula**[8] to help students relate to future patients.

So learning through play, creativity, and self-expression can benefit students of all ages. It has been proven to improve academic results and increase employability; it can also aid social and emotional development and help to build healthy societies. Simply put, it is something from which we all stand to gain.

4	**elective**	*adj.*	chosen rather than required
5	**impractical**	*adj.*	not useful; not easily put into practice
6	**prescribed**	*adj.*	advised or recommended
7	**module**	*n.*	one of the units that together make a complete course, taught especially at a college or university
8	**curriculum**	*n.*	(pl. curricula) the subjects studied in a school, college, etc., and what each subject includes

COMPREHENSION CHECK-UPS

1. According to paragraph 2, what is NOT true of Finnish education?

   a. Children don't begin to formally study until they are seven.

   b. Exams are seen as less important than in other countries.

   c. Students are not required to take arts and music in secondary school.

   d. Children must study a minimum number of hours of arts and music weekly.

2. What is true about Finnish people, according to paragraph 3?

   a. They have recently started paying higher taxes.

   b. They have a fast-growing population.

   c. They are confident and work well in teams.

   d. They tend to be relatively happy.

3. Read paragraph 3. What kinds of school activities help develop the four Cs?

   ____

   ____

4. What can be inferred from paragraph 3?

   a. Finnish children develop later than other children.

   b. Finland's system might not work everywhere.

   c. Education rankings are usually biased.

   d. Rich people tend to be more creative.

5. According to paragraph 4, all of the following are true of education in the UK EXCEPT _______.

   a. schools that focus on creative learning charge a lot of money

   b. there is not a lot of funding for the arts in ordinary schools

   c. students are choosing not to study art because of poor pay in the field

   d. students can stop taking arts and music-related classes at age fourteen

6. Read paragraph 4. How is funding for the arts in the UK described?

____

____

7. What is true about students, according to paragraph 5?

a. Schools that teach arts attract more students from poor backgrounds.
b. Less-wealthy students tend to do better than others at creative subjects.
c. Creative schools give less-wealthy students more time to study for exams.
d. Creative subjects encourage less-wealthy students to stay in school.

8. In paragraph 5, why does the author use the phrase "number-one attribute"?

a. To clarify which subject in the arts is most important
b. To describe how companies' priorities are changing
c. To define what businesses value in potential staff
d. To explain which qualities leaders need to have

9. According to paragraph 6, what did Grant Wood believe about teaching art?

a. It is not possible to teach because art is a talent.
b. It is a possible means to improve human well-being.
c. It is crucial to improving academic results and employability.
d. It is linked to people achieving more academically.

10. Which statement best restates the sentence, "It can also build emotional intelligence and encourage empathy: leading universities such as Harvard and Columbia now include art lectures and modules like painting in their medical schools' curricula to help students relate to future patients." from paragraph 6?

a. Reputable colleges use art to teach medical students emotional intelligence.
b. Medical students learn to paint because it teaches them about the body.
c. Medical students are required to learn about the importance of art therapy.
d. Universities are teaching arts to doctors because it helps them to relax.

MAPPING IDEAS

Read the sentences and match them to the best points of view in the graphic organizer.

STATEMENTS

1. When they do arrive at school, their first "pre-primary" year is defined mainly by play, and it is not until seven that a more formal academic curriculum is introduced.
2. As their education continues, rigid, didactic teaching and standardized tests are given far less significance than in many nations.
3. In fact, for each student at an ordinary school in the UK, the 2021 budget allows just £9.40 ($12.79) for art and music education each year.
4. According to research, in schools with low participation in the arts, around twenty-two percent of low socio-economic status children do not graduate.
5. The arts themselves can also contribute to nations financially. Today, the UK's culture industry adds around £11 billion to the economy.
6. Simply put, it is something from which we all stand to gain.

POINTS OF VIEW	
A. NEUTRAL	**B. BIASED**

VOCABULARY REVIEW

Fill in the blanks with the correct words from the box. Change the form if needed.

orient	**cooperative**	**availability**	**illogical**
contribute	**culture**	**tangibly**	**prescribed**

1. London has a rich ________________; it boasts great architecture, museums, and restaurants.
2. The manager said the team needed to be ________________ and talk to each other more.
3. It is ________________ to fire Jim since he is the best salesman at the company.
4. The essay was written to the ________________ rules: 10,000 words long and in Chicago style.
5. During the war, people's health suffered because the ________________ of fresh fruit was low.
6. There are magazines specifically ________________ to every possible interest—sports, health, entertainment, etc.
7. The school newspaper editor asked ten students to ________________ one piece of writing each.
8. The new policy ________________ benefited the poor by providing great assistance.

CRITICAL-THINKING SKILL

Finding Fallacies

Fallacies use faulty reasoning to create an argument. They can make an argument sound more persuasive than it really is. Writers can use them intentionally or unintentionally.
In a valid argument, if the premises are true, then it's impossible for the conclusion to be false.

For example:

(1) Everyone in this class is either the teacher or a student.

(2) Amy is in this class, and (3) she is not a teacher.

(4) Therefore, Amy must be a student.

In a fallacious argument, the conclusion may be false even if the premises are true. For example:

(1) Everyone in Amy's class is a college student.

(2) I am not in Amy's class.

(3) Therefore, I am not a college student.

Finding fallacies will help readers evaluate arguments and make strong objections.

Read the arguments. Then complete the activity. Discuss your responses with a partner.

1 **PREMISE 1** Finnish children have a creative education.

PREMISE 2 Finnish children achieve high grades in examinations.

CONCLUSION Creative education improves grades.

Explain why the argument is a fallacy.

____

____

2 **PREMISE 1** UK schools are cutting funding for the arts.

PREMISE 2 Fewer children are choosing to study arts.

CONCLUSION Children are not studying arts because there is no equipment.

Explain why the argument is a fallacy.

____

____

IDEAS IN DISCUSSION

1. What are your favorite subjects in school? In those subjects, when do you need creativity?

2. What are some memorable classes you have had? How did they influence you?

3. What creative subject do you think is the most beneficial to study?

4. In your opinion, should your government prioritize funding for practical subjects over the arts? Why or why not?

5. According to the reading, seventy-seven percent of employers rank creativity as the number one attitude they are looking for in new employees. Why do you think creativity is valued so much by employers in your country, too?

IDEAS IN WRITING

1. Write a paragraph about studying creative subjects and the reasons why it could be valuable to individuals and societies.

2. American painter Grant Wood states, "The aim of art education in public schools is not to make more professional artists but to teach people to live happier, fuller lives." Do you agree with this statement? Write your opinion, providing three reasons to support your viewpoint.

3. Reflect on your personal experiences with art or creative subjects in school. How did they impact your overall education or well-being? Write about your experiences within 250–300 words.

4. Finland's education system emphasizes play and creativity, leading to both academic success and reported happiness. Do you think this approach could also work in your country? Why or why not?

5. If you could design an education system for your country, what changes or adjustments would you make to improve the curriculum you experienced in school, such as subjects, teaching methods, creative activities, or overall balance?

ENVIRONMENT

UNIT 6-1 Profits or the Planet

Scan and find the tracks.

READING 1

SKILLS

Reading Skill:
Asking Questions While Reading

Critical-Thinking Skill:
Identifying Premises and Conclusions

WARM-UP QUESTIONS

1. Do you buy eco-friendly products? Why or why not?

2. Who is responsible for making sure companies treat employees well?

3. How do you think customers (like you and your family) can encourage businesses to care about the environment and people?

4. When companies say they care about the environment or social issues, do you think they really mean it, or are they doing it for other reasons?

5. Should the government do more to encourage companies to care more about the environment?

BEFORE YOU READ

Rank the statements from 1 (most agree with) to 6 (least agree with). Discuss your rankings with a partner.

________ I want a job that pays a lot of money.

________ I want a job that helps people.

________ I want a job that is friendly to the environment.

________ I want a job at a place that treats its employees well.

________ I want a job at a large corporation.

________ I want a job with a good public image.

VOCABULARY PREVIEW

1 Read the sentences. Circle the words closest in meaning to the words in bold.

1. Corporate Social Responsibility is a popular **concept** in management.
   a. creation　　b. image　　c. idea

2. This US coffee company tries to buy its supplies **ethically**.
   a. enthusiastically　　b. properly　　c. efficiently

3. Customers demand social and environmental protections, so companies must include them in their **strategy**.
   a. policy　　b. plan　　c. purpose

4. Many companies use CSR **initiatives** to improve their public image.
   a. encounters　　b. skills　　c. programs

5. Many companies find that the extra production costs are not **recovered** by more sales.
   a. regained　　b. dropped　　c. increased

6. A maker of **consumer** goods found that most people don't try to buy eco-friendly products.
   a. camper　　b. marketer　　c. user

7. A typical **investor** in a company wants to make as much profit as possible.
   a. owner　　b. administrator　　c. officer

8. Public opinion is changing corporate **attitudes** about CSR.
   a. images　　b. views　　c. policies

2 Match the words in section 1 above to their definitions below.

________ : a feeling or opinion about something or a way of behaving that is caused by this

________ : a principle or idea

________ : someone who buys goods or services for personal use

________ : in a way that is morally right or that relates to moral principles

________ : a plan or process to achieve something or solve problems

________ : a person who puts money into something in order to make a profit

________ : to get back something lost or spent

________ : a detailed plan for achieving success in situations such as war, politics, or business

PROFITS OR THE PLANET

Track 11

1. **Reading Skill: Asking Questions While Reading**
   Actively ask questions about the text and think about the answers as you read. This helps you understand, make connections, and make inferences about the text better.
2. **Critical-Thinking Skill: Identifying Premises and Conclusions**
   An argument includes premises (reasons) and a conclusion. Reasons are sometimes indicated with expressions such as *because, since, thus, therefore,* etc.

Corporate Social Responsibility (CSR) is a management concept that means companies include social and environmental concerns in their operations and hold themselves responsible for their actions. For example, the Starbucks Coffee Company has set and met many CSR **milestones**[1]. They've reached ninety-nine percent ethically-sourced coffee and contributed millions of hours of community service. CSR has become an increasingly important part of corporate strategies since much of the public demands social and environmental protection. Yet, some people still argue that CSR is a misleading, **wasteful**[2], and unproductive practice.

The benefit for companies that take part in CSR initiatives is that it boosts brand value. Companies with CSR initiatives get more sympathetic treatment in the media. This is because people believe that CSR-committed companies care more for their customers. But there is good reason to believe that some companies don't take CSR seriously and only do the minimum needed to benefit without taking on extra expenses. Take, for example, the Volkswagen **emissions**[3] scandal in 2015. The United States Environmental Protection Agency found that Volkswagen had knowingly broken the rules in the Clean Air Act by programming its cars to turn on emissions controls only during laboratory testing. This happened after the company had gained lots of positive publicity for its "clean" engines. By the time Volkswagen was caught, this software had been installed in over 11 million cars worldwide.

1	**milestone**	*n.*	an important point or step in a project, process, or development
2	**wasteful**	*adj.*	using or taking more of something than is needed, causing it to be wasted
3	**emissions**	*n.*	something that is sent out or emitted, such as gas or energy

Another criticism of CSR initiatives is they're expensive. Maintaining safety, eco-friendliness, and responsibility costs money. Almost all companies judge their production process by doing a cost-benefit analysis (CBA). A CBA is an organized way of estimating the strengths and weaknesses of a product, service, or strategy. Unfortunately, many companies find that the increase in production cost isn't recovered by sales when adopting CSR policies. A poll in New Zealand found that four out of five people believed climate change to be an important issue. Yet an international study of 20,000 customers by consumer-goods supplier Unilever found that only one in three people actually chose to buy eco-friendly brands. Thus, people's words aren't very reliable for predicting their buying habits.

CSR initiatives can also be **demotivating**[4]. Certainly, there are companies whose practices give employees a sense of pride by being environmentally and socially responsible. However, this is not true for all. Typically, employees that reduce profits are punished for it. For example, a factory manager is more likely to be punished for slowing down production to follow safety rules than to be rewarded. Much of this is because avoiding disaster isn't as easily noticed as solving problems. To illustrate, imagine an employee working in the oil industry. This person is less likely to be rewarded for having no oil spills than an employee who fixes an oil spill incident quickly.

Perhaps the biggest conflict at the heart of CSR is whether or not companies should even be held responsible for regulating themselves. Nobel prize-winning economist Milton Friedman argued in a 1970 essay titled "A Friedman Doctrine: The Social Responsibility of Business is to Increase Its Profits" that a company has no social responsibility to the public or society. His theory states that a corporation's only responsibility is to meet the desires of its employers (shareholders). And since many investors want to maximize profits, people who run corporations have to avoid policies that reduce profits. Friedman believed that the only appropriate agents of social causes are individuals. To illustrate, consider fast-food chains. Are those chains responsible for **obesity**[5]? Are they accountable for customers littering? For those who support Friedman's theory, the answer would be no.

Although there are many criticisms of CSR policies, public demand is starting to change many corporations' attitudes about the part they have to play. In fact, many companies have adopted a **quantifiable**[6] set of standards known as environmental, social, and corporate **governance**[7] criteria, or ESG, to communicate to investors their companies' commitment to social responsibility. This set of standards forces companies to regulate their commitments in measurable ways while giving them a financial incentive to do so. But is this meaningful change or just more corporate **jargon**[8]? Time will tell.

4	**demotivating**	*adj.*	making someone less pleased with doing work or a task
5	**obesity**	*n.*	the condition of being extremely fat to the point of danger to one's health
6	**quantifiable**	*adj.*	able to be measured
7	**governance**	*n.*	the way that organizations or countries are managed at the highest level and the systems for doing this
8	**jargon**	*n.*	usually used negatively: the language used by a particular group of people for certain activities

COMPREHENSION CHECK-UPS

1. According to paragraph 1, all of the following ideas about CSR are true EXCEPT _______.

a. it's a management concept that involves social and environmental concerns
b. it's an important strategy since the public demands environmental protection
c. it's an unpopular management concept that has been replaced in recent years
d. it's an idea that some people oppose because they believe it is misleading

2. According to paragraph 2, why are CSR initiatives being criticized?

a. They actually do little to boost brand value.
b. They force companies to break government rules.
c. They're used dishonestly by companies.
d. They're too expensive to do properly.

3. According to paragraph 3, why are CBAs important for corporations?

a. They calculate the risks and rewards of important decisions.
b. They provide vital information about their customer base.
c. They help make the production process more efficient.
d. They are used to help sales recover from poor planning.

4. Read paragraph 3 and write the evidence that people's words aren't very helpful in predicting their shopping choices.

____

____

5. According to paragraph 4, all of the following are true about CSR initiatives EXCEPT _______.

a. some employees take pride in working for a company with CSR initiatives
b. they're motivational because CSR initiatives reward workers who maintain safety
c. companies punish workers who reduce profits regardless of CSR initiatives
d. CSR initiatives can be demotivating since they don't reward prevention

6. **According to paragraph 5, Milton Friedman believed that an executive's sole responsibility was toward whom?**

a. The public
b. The investor
c. The customer
d. The government

7. **In paragraph 5, why does the author mention obesity?**

a. To give an example of fast-food chains which have caused social problems
b. To give an example of Milton Friedman's theory on public health
c. To give an example of a concern that investors have regarding their customers
d. To give an example of a social issue that Friedman would not consider a company's responsibility

8. **What can be inferred about Milton Friedman from paragraph 5?**

a. He would support a movement to shut down fast-food restaurants.
b. He did not consider the environment a major concern.
c. He wanted only socially aware people to run companies.
d. He would blame obesity on individual choices.

9. **Which statement best restates the sentence, "In fact, many companies have adopted a quantifiable set of standards known as environmental, social, and corporate governance criteria, or ESG, to communicate to investors their companies' commitment to social responsibility." from paragraph 6?**

a. Many companies are using a measurable standard to show they're invested in social responsibility.
b. Many companies are partnering with other companies that are invested in social responsibility.
c. Many companies have reduced their commitments to ESG standards.
d. Many companies adopt the ESG standards that their investors have selected.

10. **Read paragraph 6 and think of other examples of corporate jargon.**

____

____

MAPPING IDEAS

Read the statements and match them with the correct questions to complete each part of the graphic organizer.

PROFITS OR THE PLANET		
Why are some people opposed to CSR practices and initiatives?		
1. ______________		
Why would a company like Volkswagen knowingly break the Clean Air Act?	**What did Unilever discover about consumer spending habits?**	**How can CSR initiatives be demotivating for employees?**
2. ______________	3. ______________	4. ______________

STATEMENTS

a. They found that people say they want social responsibility but are unwilling to pay for it.
b. They believe that they're misleading, wasteful, and unproductive.
c. They believe that a corporation's top priority should be profits.
d. They wanted to benefit from the positive attention without investing a lot of money.
e. They can make people feel underappreciated since avoiding problems isn't easily recognized.

VOCABULARY REVIEW

Fill in the blanks with the correct words from the box. Change the form if needed.

strategy	recover	attitude	jargon
emission	investor	consumer	initiative

1. ______________ should research a company thoroughly before trusting it with their money.
2. The lost data was ______________ by a technician who backed up the project last month.
3. The employer was worried about his employee's ______________ after being denied a raise.
4. The company formed a(n) ______________ to become more competitive in the market.
5. Cars need to be tested to ensure their ______________ are within government regulations.
6. "Best practice" is ______________ for saying something is the best way to do something.
7. As part of a large public health ______________, the government provides free flu shots.
8. When prices rise, ______________ tend to shop less overall.

CRITICAL-THINKING SKILL

Identifying Premises and Conclusions

Arguments include reasons called premises and a conclusion. Writers might sometimes state their conclusion before their premises. Identifying the premises and conclusion will help you better understand a writer's argument. For example:

People who care about their health should exercise daily (conclusion).

Research shows that people who exercise thirty minutes or more a day have less risk of developing heart disease and cancer (premise).

1 **Read the excerpts from the reading. Each contains an argument. For each part in the excerpt, circle P for premise or C for a conclusion.**

STATEMENTS	
1. (P / C)	A poll in New Zealand found that four out of five people believed climate change to be an important issue.
(P / C)	Yet, an international study of 20,000 customers by consumer-goods supplier Unilever found that only one in three people actually chose to buy eco-friendly brands.
(P / C)	Thus, people's words aren't very reliable for predicting their buying habits.
2. (P / C)	Although there are many criticisms of CSR policies, public demand is starting to change many corporations' attitudes about the part they have to play.
(P / C)	In fact, many companies have adopted a quantifiable set of standards known as environmental, social, and governance criteria, or ESG, to communicate to investors their companies' commitment to social responsibility.
(P / C)	This set of standards forces companies to regulate their commitments in measurable ways while giving them a financial incentive to do so.

IDEAS IN DISCUSSION

1. What are some common ways that companies mistreat their workers?
2. What are some common ways that companies harm the environment?
3. Do you agree with Milton Friedman's idea on companies and profits? Why or why not?
4. How would you define Corporate Social Responsibility (CSR) in your own words? Why do you think it's important for companies to consider CSR?
5. Should businesses be responsible for problems caused by their products, such as pollution or health issues? Why or why not?

IDEAS IN WRITING

1. Write a paragraph about Corporate Social Responsibility and whether or not companies should engage in it.
2. Describe the criticism that some companies only participate in CSR to improve their image. Do you think this is true for most companies? Why or why not?
3. Discuss how cultural values and norms can influence the types of CSR initiatives that are effective in different countries.
4. Describe a situation where you think a company should or shouldn't be held responsible for the social or environmental impact of their products.
5. Discuss how consumer choices can influence businesses to adopt CSR policies. What actions can people take to make a difference?

ENVIRONMENT

UNIT 6-2 The French Model and the Future of Nuclear Power

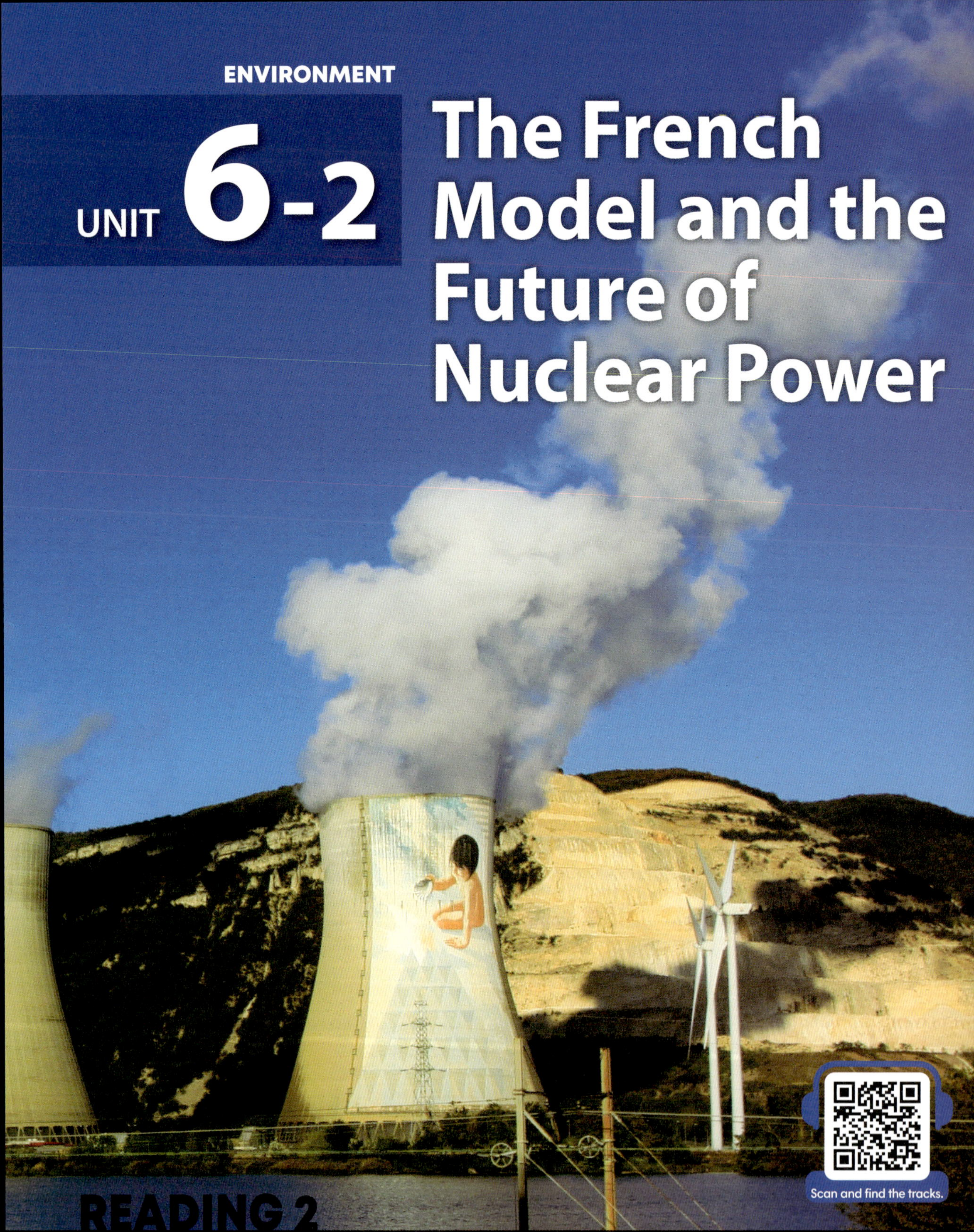

Scan and find the tracks.

READING 2

SKILLS

Reading Skill:

Critical-Thinking Skill:

WARM-UP QUESTIONS

1. Why are many people afraid of using nuclear power?
2. How does your country produce the majority of its energy?
3. Can you name some examples of renewable energy sources?
4. Why is it important to think about the long-term effects of using fossil fuels?
5. If you could design a new way to generate electricity, what would it look like? How would it work?

BEFORE YOU READ

Read the statements. Check (✓) whether you agree or disagree with each statement. Discuss your answers with a partner.

	Strongly disagree	Disagree somewhat	Agree somewhat	Strongly agree
1. I use a lot of electricity in my day-to-day life.				
2. Electricity is expensive in my country.				
3. Nuclear energy can be used safely.				
4. We should eliminate all nuclear energy.				
5. All countries should prioritize green energy solutions.				

VOCABULARY PREVIEW

1 Read the sentences. Circle the words closest in meaning to the words in bold.

1. France will spend money to ensure the sites that nuclear power stations **occupy** are safe.
   a. attract b. possess c. inhabit

2. France's **reliance** on nuclear power means it is very green and has low carbon emissions.
   a. dependence b. insistence c. assurance

3. Many European countries are choosing **projects** which reduce emissions with renewables.
   a. tactics b. ventures c. intentions

4. Solar and wind energy are **unreliable** because they need certain conditions to work efficiently.
   a. pointless b. reductive c. questionable

5. Nuclear plants deliver **constant** power for as long as forty years.
   a. dedicated b. reliable c. steady

6. Today, we even have the ability to extend the working **duration** of nuclear power stations.
   a. persistence b. lifetime c. survival

7. The US government cannot agree on how to **secure** nuclear waste at one of its former power stations.
   a. guard b. fasten c. assure

8. Instead of closing down nuclear power stations, we should invest and begin a new **chapter**.
   a. measure b. topic c. era

2 Match the words in bold in section 1 above to their definitions below.

________ : a period that is part of a larger amount of time during which something happens

________ : happening all the time

________ : the time during which something exists or lasts

________ : to take up a place or extent in space

________ : a planned piece of work that has a specific purpose and that usually requires a lot of time

________ : the state of depending on or trusting in something or someone

________ : to get something, sometimes with difficulty

________ : not to be trusted or depended on

THE FRENCH MODEL AND THE FUTURE OF NUCLEAR POWER

Track 12

1. **Reading Skill: Understanding Cause and Effect**
   Cause-and-effect relationships show a result that is directly influenced by an action or event. Writers often signal these relationships with words such as *so, thus, since, therefore, because (of), as a result, due to,* etc.

2. **Critical-Thinking Skill: Identifying Cause and Effect**
   It is important to recognize how different ideas in a passage relate to one another, and one of the most common relationships between ideas is cause and effect.

As the effects of climate change become increasingly apparent, many countries are looking to develop innovative forms of renewable energy, including wind, solar, and **hydropower**[1]. However, the world already has an advanced, clean, and efficient means of producing large amounts of energy: nuclear power.

France has long realized the practical benefits of nuclear power as an alternative to fossil fuels such as coal, oil, and gas. These substances are hard to produce or extract, are concentrated in certain parts of the planet, and are in limited supply. In 1973, following the Yom Kippur War, Saudi Arabia cut off oil supplies to some nations, and the price of oil skyrocketed from $3 per **barrel**[2] to $15 in a single day, and then $40 by the end of the decade. Realizing the need for independence, the French government under Prime Minister Pierre Messmer drew up the "Messmer Plan," an investment program that would involve the construction of 80 nuclear power plants by 1985 and 170 by the year 2000. The plan was a success. Today, as much as seventy percent of France's energy needs are met by nuclear power. In addition, the country is now largely protected from oil crises and free from **dependence**[3] on foreign fossil fuels.

French residents are regularly reminded of the benefits of nuclear power every time their electricity bill arrives. At only $0.22 per kilowatt-hour in 2020, their electricity currently remains

[1] **hydropower** *n.* electricity supplied by water power
[2] **barrel** *n.* a round, bulging drum that is taller than its breadth
[3] **dependence** *n.* state of being controlled by something else or needing support from someone else

among the cheapest in the world. In Denmark, the cost is around $0.34, and in Germany, it is closer to $0.40; these countries still primarily rely on fossil fuels. The costs of fossil fuels are not only financial: the rate of worker deaths within the oil industry is 263 times higher than those in nuclear energy. Accidents like those at Chernobyl are alarming, but they are infrequent. A fitting comparison could be made with air travel—it seems risky, and when accidents do take place, they receive huge amounts of **coverage**[4], but it is statistically far less dangerous than traveling by bus, car, boat, or train. In any case, to calm the public's fears, France announced in 2012 that it would spend $13.2 billion on safety upgrades to its reactors and the sites they occupy.

Moreover, reliance on nuclear power means that France is one of the greenest countries on Earth. Its carbon emissions are one-tenth of those in Germany and the UK and one-thirteenth of those in Denmark. These countries are attempting to reduce carbon emissions by focusing on wind and solar projects; however, few modern renewable forms of energy can match nuclear power for its low levels of pollution. For each gigawatt-hour generated (the amount of energy roughly needed to power 160 homes in the EU annually), a nuclear power plant produces three tons of carbon. Running a **wind farm**[5] emits four tons for the same amount of power, and a solar array emits five tons. Hydropower, meanwhile, puts far more carbon into the air: thirty-four tons per gigawatt-hour.

Renewable forms of energy like wind and solar primarily rely on unpredictable and unreliable weather conditions that are only found in certain regions and at certain times of the year. Once built, a nuclear power station quietly produces constant power for a lifetime of up to forty years, and today we have the technology to extend this duration. In fact, the decommissioning, or closing, of nuclear power stations can raise difficult questions. At San Onofre, California, a nuclear power station was decommissioned in 2013. However, by 2021, federal authorities had still not agreed on how to properly secure the dangerous nuclear waste that remains on-site. Without workable plans for their **closure**[6], stations like San Onofre might as well have been safely upgraded.

Nuclear power has the potential to solve many problems. It can slow climate change significantly by providing a greener alternative to fossil fuels, and, unlike many renewables, it is a proven way to produce energy consistently and in large quantities; it is also safer than many people suggest. Rather than **consigning**[7] nuclear power to the **scrap heap**[8] —which carries its own risks—now could be the perfect time to reassess, reinvest, and begin a new chapter for nuclear power.

4	**coverage**	*n.*	material within the scope of a discussion or report
5	**wind farm**	*n.*	an area of land with a cluster of wind turbines for producing energy
6	**closure**	*n.*	the shutting down or closing of a thing
7	**consign**	*v.*	to give, transfer, or deliver into the hands or control of another
8	**scrap heap**	*n.*	the place where useless things are discarded

COMPREHENSION CHECK-UPS

1. According to paragraph 1, what is a common response to climate change?
   a. Improving existing nuclear power infrastructure
   b. Mixing nuclear with renewable energy sources
   c. Replacing renewable energy with nuclear power
   d. Investigating innovative renewable energy sources

2. According to paragraph 2, what happened in France in the 1970s?
   a. The country's government declared independence.
   b. The government acted to control the price of oil.
   c. A plan was enacted to deal with the rising price of oil.
   d. A Saudi oil company set up its own power stations.

3. Read paragraph 2 and write why fossil fuels are not a practical solution to energy needs.

   ____

   ____

4. What can be inferred from paragraph 2?
   a. France and Saudi Arabia agreed on the price of oil in the 1970s.
   b. France was an important ally of Saudi Arabia during the Yom Kippur War.
   c. Pierre Messmer wanted to try to seize control of global oil prices.
   d. Saudi Arabia did not view France as a friend during the early 1970s.

5. According to paragraph 3, all of the following are true EXCEPT ______.
   a. figures show that nuclear power is as dangerous as air travel
   b. in France, nuclear energy keeps the cost of energy down
   c. the French government has announced safety upgrades
   d. oil is more dangerous for workers than nuclear power

6. In paragraph 3, why does the author use the phrase "In any case"?

a. To imply that France is acting slowly to address the risks
b. To say that France is being proactive about safety precautions
c. To tell us that nuclear power is less dangerous than it seems
d. To suggest that nuclear power is expensive to make safe

7. According to paragraph 4, which is NOT true?

a. Wind power produces less carbon than hydropower.
b. Hydropower plants emit more carbon than nuclear plants.
c. France's carbon emissions are lower than those of Germany and the UK.
d. Solar power generates fewer emissions than power from wind.

8. Read paragraph 4 and write how some nations attempt to bring down their carbon output.

___

___

9. According to paragraph 5, why is nuclear power advantageous?

a. It is financially difficult to upgrade renewable energy sites.
b. Renewable energy is inconsistent and not viable in all locations.
c. Nuclear sites last longer than wind farms and solar arrays.
d. Nuclear power stations can easily be decommissioned.

10. Which statement best restates the sentence, "Once built, a nuclear power station quietly produces constant power for a lifetime of up to forty years, and today we have the technology to extend this duration." from paragraph 5?

a. New nuclear technology is emerging, and it could extend the life of our nuclear plants.
b. Nuclear power stations produce reliable energy, but they still have limited lifetimes.
c. Nuclear power plants can work well for forty years, and this period can be increased.
d. Newly built nuclear power plants are expected to continue operating for forty years.

MAPPING IDEAS

Read the causes and match them to the best effect.

CAUSES		EFFECTS
Saudi Arabia refuses to send its oil to some countries during the Yom Kippur War.	→	**1.** ______________
The Messmer Plan has France build many nuclear power stations domestically.	→	**2.** ______________
France uses nuclear power to produce 70.6 percent of its energy cheaply.	→	**3.** ______________
A few alarming nuclear accidents have occurred.	→	**4.** ______________
Nuclear power produces less carbon than modern renewable sources of energy.	→	**5.** ______________

EFFECTS

a. Electricity becomes more affordable.
b. France invests in improving safety at nuclear facilities.
c. France works toward energy independence.
d. Nuclear power contributes less to global warming.
e. The price of oil rises.

VOCABULARY REVIEW

Fill in the blanks with the correct words from the box. Change the form if needed.

occupy	**reliance**	**project**	**unreliable**
constant	**secure**	**coverage**	**closure**

1. Although it is excellent, few people know of the film because it has received very little media ______________.
2. Manufacturing companies need to reduce their ______________ on fossil fuels.
3. The ______________ of the factory has left thousands of people without work.
4. My family's car is fifteen years old and has begun to be slightly ______________; I think we need a new one!
5. Stopping climate change will require the ______________ efforts of the international community.
6. Architects Olufsen and Ball are working on an exciting new ______________ in New York City.
7. Each night, Nelly uses a padlock and chain to ______________ her jewelry store.
8. The Embassy of Denmark ______________ two floors of a tall building near the palace.

CRITICAL-THINKING SKILL

Identifying Cause and Effect

It is important to recognize how different ideas in a passage relate to one another, and one of the most common relationships between ideas is cause and effect. There are several different combinations of cause and effect. Here are the main ones:

(1) One cause can explain many effects (effect-focused)

(2) One effect may be the result of several causes (cause-focused)

(3) Chain of causation

1 Read the text. Then answer the questions.

The anti-nuclear movement has a long history in Germany. In 1975, thousands of protestors gathered at the site of a nuclear power plant in Whyl and eventually succeeded in stopping its construction. Larger demonstrations took place in several German cities in 1979 after the accident at Three Mile Island in the US. Additional protests against the processing and storage of nuclear waste followed, contributing to the founding of the Green Party in 1980. The disaster at Chernobyl, Ukraine, in 1986, also influenced German public opinion, and no new nuclear power plants have been built in the country since 1989. However, energy prices now have many Germans rethinking the value of nuclear power. The country—which relies heavily on coal and natural gas—pays the highest prices for energy in Europe, and those prices are still rising. One recent study showed an eleven-percent increase in support for nuclear power since 2018.

1. What did protesters do to stop the construction of a nuclear power plant?

2. What happened in Germany after the Three Mile Island incident?

3. What important political effect did anti-nuclear feelings have in Germany in 1980?

4. What is a likely reason for the recent increase in pro-nuclear opinion?

5. What kind of cause-and-effect relationship is being shown in the passage?

IDEAS IN DISCUSSION

1. Do you think it's possible to use nuclear power safely?

2. Which argument for investing in nuclear power do you find the most convincing?

3. What would make renewable energy more attractive and get people to invest in it?

4. How can nuclear power contribute to energy independence for nations?

5. What role, if any, should governments play in supporting the development and regulation of nuclear power?

IDEAS IN WRITING

1. Write a paragraph about energy problems in your country and how they can be solved.

2. Imagine you are an environmental policy advisor. Write a paragraph advocating for or against increased nuclear energy investment to combat climate change.

3. Reflect on the trade-offs between energy reliability, cost, and environmental impact. Which energy source do you think strikes the best balance, and why?

4. Propose a solution to a specific challenge facing the nuclear power industry, such as the problem of nuclear waste disposal or the need to improve public acceptance of nuclear power.

5. Explain how energy independence can benefit a country economically and politically, using France's response to the 1973 oil crisis as an example.

SPORTS

UNIT 7-1 Sport or Art?

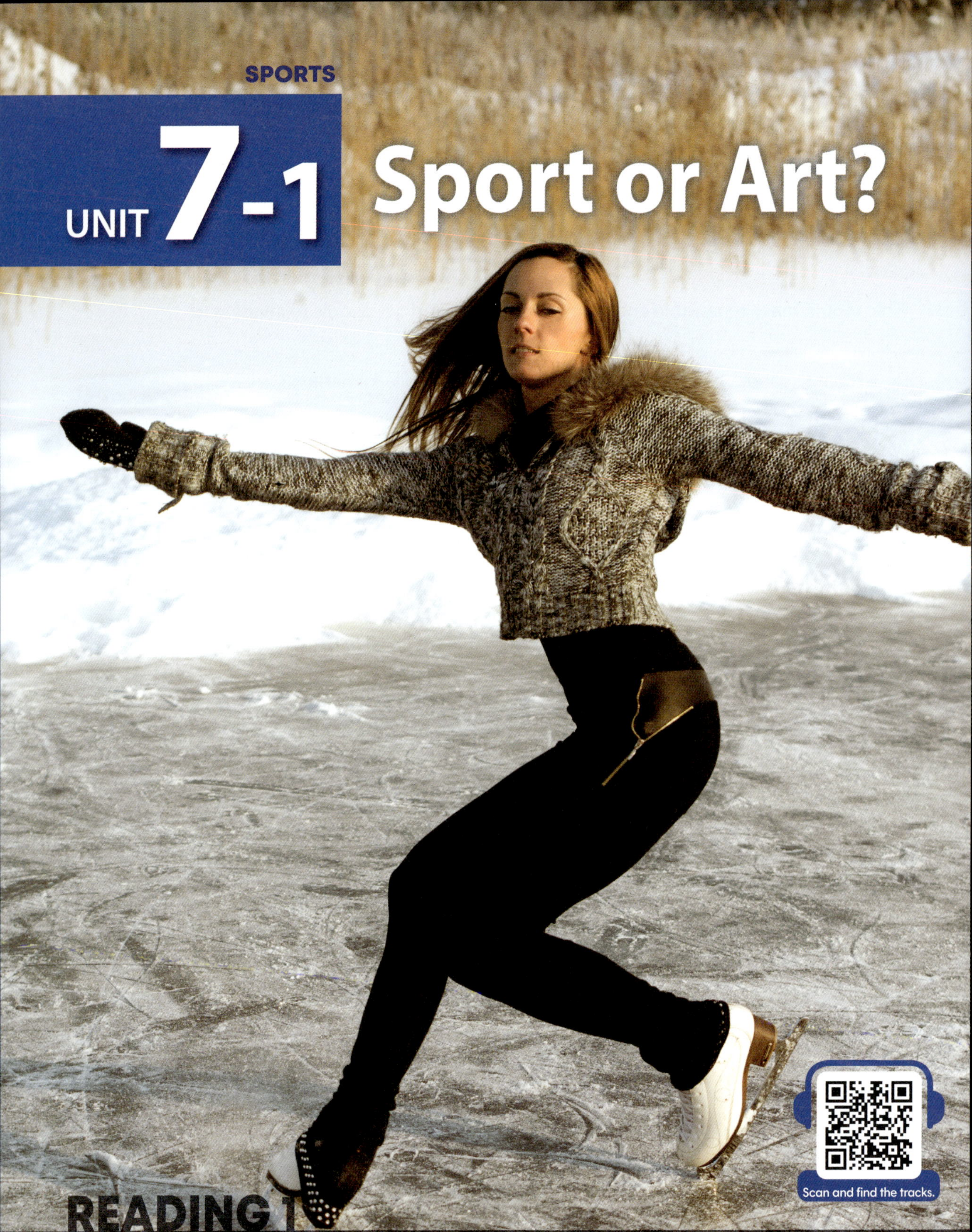

Scan and find the tracks.

READING 1

SKILLS

Reading Skill:
Setting a Purpose for Reading

Critical-Thinking Skill:
Detecting the Author's Purpose

WARM-UP QUESTIONS

1. Which sports do you think are the most enjoyable to watch? Why?
2. Have you ever felt strong emotions while playing or watching sports? Explain.
3. Do you think sports and art have any similarities? What are they?
4. Who is someone in sports or art that inspires you, and what do you admire about them?
5. Which do you think is more important in society: sports or art? Why?

BEFORE YOU READ

Read the statements. Check (✓) whether you agree or disagree with each statement. Discuss your answers with a partner.

	Strongly disagree	Disagree somewhat	Agree somewhat	Strongly agree
1. I enjoy watching Olympic competitions.				
2. Everyone should play at least one sport while growing up.				
3. Figure skating is more like dancing than a sport.				
4. Being a great athlete is about more than physical ability.				
5. Sports are a good way to learn about teamwork.				

VOCABULARY PREVIEW

1 Read the sentences. Circle the words closest in meaning to the words in bold.

1. Thrilling music **accompanies** Olympic figure skating routines.
   a. goes with b. distracts from c. comes after
2. A **panel** of judges determines the skaters' scores.
   a. supervisor b. committee c. opinion
3. The **domain** of sports includes more than just athletic ability.
   a. power b. area c. appeal
4. Art and sports actually **overlap** in some ways.
   a. are competitive b. are unnecessary c. are similar
5. The scoring for the event **ranges** from zero to ten.
   a. varies b. begins c. displays
6. There are **arbitrary** factors in all sports, such as a bad call by an umpire.
   a. fair b. precise c. inconsistent
7. Beauty is not outside the **scope** of sports.
   a. possibility b. field c. background
8. Do you think figure skating should be **categorized** as a sport?
   a. labeled b. rejected c. improved

2 Match the words in bold in section 1 above to their definitions below.

________ : to happen or exist while something else is happening

________ : based on or determined by an individual's preference rather than necessity or intrinsic nature

________ : to put into a group or category; to classify

________ : an area of knowledge or activity

________ : to have something in common

________ : a group of people selected for some service

________ : to have an upper and a lower limit in amount, number, etc.

________ : the extent of treatment, activity, or influence

SPORT OR ART?

Track 13

1. **Reading Skill: Setting a Purpose for Reading**
   Set a goal before reading, such as reading for enjoyment, learning technical information, seeing a new point of view, or learning about a subject.

2. **Detecting the Author's Purpose**
   Authors write for many reasons: to inform, persuade, entertain, etc. Knowing the author's purpose helps you think critically about the reading.

It's easy to understand why women's figure skating is the most popular Olympic event. Athletes perform amazing jumps and spins accompanied by thrilling music. But a predictable debate happens every four years among sports fans. Some aren't happy about including figure skating in the Olympics because they believe it's more of an art than a "real" sport.

This view rests on the fact that figure skaters receive two different scores from a panel of judges. The technical score is based on the difficulty of the routine and whether the skater performed certain required moves correctly. The program components score depends on more subjective factors, including **choreography**[1] and "interpretation of music." That second score is the part that critics have a problem with. In 2018, a sports reporter named Edward Egros started an online argument when he tweeted that figure skating is "too **subjective**[2]" and lacks "quantifiable metrics to determine a winner." Other users pointed out that scores are, in fact, quantified precisely. But Egros was not convinced. According to him, figure skating requires impressive skills, but it's not a sport. He is mistaken, however. What he and other critics of Olympic figure skating are missing is the fact that the domains of sports and art overlap a great deal.

Take skateboarding, for example, which became an Olympic event for the first time in 2021.

[1] **choreography** *n.* the process of designing dances for a performance
[2] **subjective** *adj.* influenced by someone's beliefs or feelings instead of facts

Participants are judged on a scale ranging from zero to ten. The criteria include not only difficulty and speed but also timing and **originality**[3]. Skateboarders value the creative elements of the sport so much that many had mixed feelings about it being added to the Games. Ian Michna, a skateboard magazine publisher, explained to NBC News, "I think as a community, people were attracted to skateboarding because it was not part of something like the Olympics. . . . It was more of an artistic activity you could do on your own." But even stars like Tony Hawk have changed their minds on this point. Hawk used to oppose the "sportification" of skateboarding, but he agreed to report on the event for a US TV channel, saying that he hoped more people around the world would be encouraged to take up the sport he loves.

The great Brazilian soccer player Pelé famously called his sport o jogo bonito, or "the beautiful game." There are various ways to interpret this phrase. Soccer players' **athleticism**[4] can be amazing to watch; for example, Ronaldinho, another Brazilian star, became famous for his dance-like **footwork**[5]. Or maybe Pelé was referring to soccer's ability to surprise—anything can happen at any time. Another beautiful part of the game, as one sportswriter pointed out, is how it makes fans all over the world feel like they are a part of something: "When they go to a match and add their voice to the thousands already **chanting**[6], they feel they are making a difference."

All sports—even those that judges don't score—include some subjective or arbitrary factors. A tennis **umpire**[7] might make the wrong call. A loud fan might distract a golfer during a crucial shot. A million chance events can affect the results. Near the end of the final game of the 2016 baseball World Series, the Chicago Cubs were winning by two runs and feeling confident when the other team suddenly tied the score with a home run. Then it began to rain, and the game had to stop temporarily. Thanks to this pause, a respected older Cubs player had time to address his teammates—some of whom were crying—with an inspiring speech about teamwork and determination. The Cubs went on to score two more runs and become champions. Afterward, players told reporters that their leader's well-chosen words helped ensure their victory.

In summation, it isn't true that emotions and **aesthetics**[8] are outside the scope of sports. If you ever wonder whether figure skating should be categorized as a sport or an art form, that's something to consider. All sports are art forms. They don't just require training and skill; they also appeal to our sense of beauty and inspiration.

3	**originality**	*n.*	the quality of being interesting and different from everyone or everything else
4	**athleticism**	*n.*	skill in running, jumping, throwing, and similar sports
5	**footwork**	*n.*	the way in which the feet are used in sports or dancing, especially when it involves skill
6	**chant**	*v.*	to repeat or sing a word or phrase continuously
7	**umpire**	*n.*	a person at a sports competition who makes sure that rules are obeyed and judges if certain actions are acceptable
8	**aesthetics**	*n.*	principles concerned with the nature and appreciation of beauty

COMPREHENSION CHECK-UPS

1. According to paragraphs 1 and 2, which is NOT true about women's Olympic figure skating?
   a. It is the favorite event among Olympic fans.
   b. It includes certain moves that skaters must perform.
   c. It is judged by both objective and subjective criteria.
   d. It is being criticized because of its technical score.

2. Which of the following is true according to paragraph 2?
   a. The "program components" score includes the routine's creative aspects.
   b. A sportswriter proved that figure skating scores are quantifiable.
   c. Edward Egros is not impressed with the skills of figure skaters.
   d. The author agrees with Egros's opinion on figure skating.

3. Read paragraph 2. What was the online argument about?

   ____

   ____

4. Which is stated about Ian Michna in paragraph 3?
   a. He was an Olympic skateboarder in 2021.
   b. He has been featured in skateboarding magazines.
   c. He described skateboarding as an artistic activity.
   d. He worked to add skateboarding to the Olympics.

5. Read paragraph 3 and write four things for which Olympic skateboarders are given scores.

   ____

   ____

6. Which is NOT mentioned in paragraph 4 as a reason that soccer is called "the beautiful game"?

a. The skilled movements of the players
b. The relationships between teammates
c. The unexpected outcomes
d. The emotions of the fans

7. In paragraph 4, why does the author mention Ronaldinho?

a. To emphasize the popularity of great Brazilian soccer players
b. To give an example of an athlete who plays beautifully
c. To describe how hard athletes work to become the best
d. To explain why soccer fans are devoted to their favorite players

8. According to paragraph 5, which of the following contributed to the Cubs' win?

a. A bad call by an umpire
b. A home run late in the game
c. A delay due to rain
d. A speech by a coach

9. Which statement best restates the sentence, "Near the end of the final game of the 2016 baseball World Series, the Chicago Cubs were winning by two runs and feeling confident when the other team suddenly tied the score with a home run." from paragraph 5?

a. In the final game, the Cubs were ahead until the other team hit a home run.
b. Near the end of the game, the Cubs needed two more runs to tie the score.
c. In the final game of the series, the Cubs felt pretty sure they were going to win.
d. At the end of the 2016 World Series, the Cubs were tied with the other team.

10. What can be inferred from paragraph 5?

a. Many Cubs players had been World Series champions before.
b. Cubs players took turns making speeches during the delay.
c. The Cubs were feeling discouraged when the rain started.
d. The team leader was playing his last game for the Cubs.

MAPPING IDEAS

Find the correct main idea and three supporting points. Then match them to the graphic organizer.

SPORT OR ART?		
MAIN IDEA / THESIS		
1. ______		
POINT 1	**POINT 2**	**POINT 3**
2. ______	3. ______	4. ______

a. Skateboarding does not include creativity in its scoring system.
b. Figure skaters' performances are often judged unfairly by fans.
c. Even more traditional sports like baseball include emotional elements.
d. Most skateboarders do not wish their activity to be considered a sport.
e. Soccer is both a competitive game and beautiful because of the players and fans.
f. It's wrong to think that certain sports aren't "real" sports just because they're partly subjective and artistic.

VOCABULARY REVIEW

Fill in the blanks with the correct words from the box. Change the form if needed.

athleticism	**arbitrary**	**range**	**overlap**
categorize	**originality**	**panel**	**chant**

1. Although the film is well made, it lacks ______; the entire plot is predictable.
2. The monthly rent for apartments in this building ______ from $900 to $1,200.
3. Her music is hard to ______ because it's part pop, part rock, and part hip-hop.
4. Michael Jordan was the greatest NBA player because of his ______ and a strong drive to win.
5. When the president's speech was over, the excited crowd applauded and then ______ his name.
6. A(n) ______ of managers will interview the different applicants and make a decision.
7. A teacher and a childcare worker are not the same, but their jobs ______ in some ways.
8. I don't understand why people can't drive a car until they're sixteen—that law seems so ______.

CRITICAL-THINKING SKILL

Detecting the Author's Purpose

Authors write for many reasons. Common reasons include to entertain, to inform, to explain, to teach, to persuade, and to compare and contrast. Authors can also have more than one purpose.

Read the excerpts. Evaluate them with a partner and answer the questions.

1 This view rests on the fact that figure skaters receive two different scores from a panel of judges. The technical score is based on the difficulty of the routine and whether the skater performed certain required moves correctly. The program component score depends on more subjective factors, including choreography and "interpretation of music." That second score is the part that critics have a problem with.

PURPOSE Circle the purpose. Then underline the sentence that most clearly illustrates the purpose.

a. To entertain b. To compare and contrast c. To persuade d. To inform

SUMMARIZE Write a short summary of the author's purpose.

____

2 All sports—even those that judges don't score—include some subjective or arbitrary factors. A tennis umpire might make the wrong call. A loud fan might distract a golfer during a crucial shot. A million chance events can affect the results.

PURPOSE Circle the purpose. Then underline the sentence that most clearly illustrates the purpose.

a. To entertain b. To compare and contrast c. To persuade d. To inform

SUMMARIZE Write a short summary of the author's purpose.

____

IDEAS IN DISCUSSION

1. Besides figure skating and skateboarding, what other sports have artistic elements?

2. Do you agree with Pelé that soccer is "the beautiful game"? Is there a different sport you would describe that way?

3. Would you rather be a great athlete or a great artist? Why?

4. Should schools prioritize sports and arts, or give them equal emphasis in education?

5. Imagine a world without sports or without art—which do you think would be harder to live without?

IDEAS IN WRITING

Opinion Writing

1. Write a paragraph expressing your opinion on whether sports and art overlap.

2. Should schools prioritize funding for sports or arts programs, or treat them equally? Make your case.

Analytical Writing

3. How do media and society portray athletes compared to artists? What impact does this have on their professions?

4. Analyze how both sports and art bring people together. Which do you think is more powerful in fostering community?

Reflective Writing

5. Which do you connect with more: sports or art? Explain why with examples from your life.

SPORTS

UNIT 7-2 For Fame and Fortune?

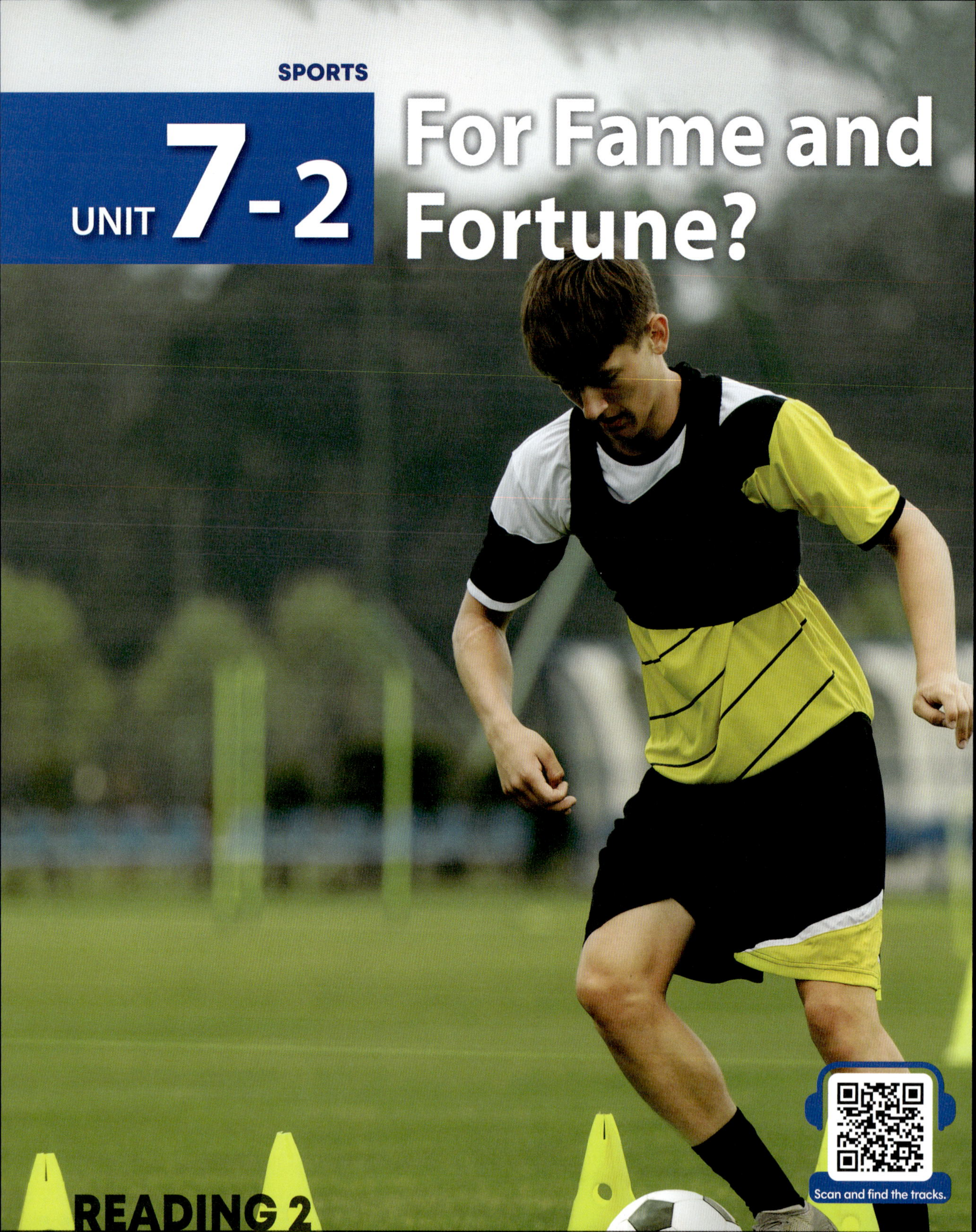

Scan and find the tracks.

READING 2

SKILLS

Reading Skill:
Setting a Purpose for Reading

Critical-Thinking Skill:
Detecting the Author's Purpose

WARM-UP QUESTIONS

1. Have you ever been part of a sports team? Which sport was it?
2. If you had the chance to be a sports star, would you take it? Why or why not?
3. If you could excel at any sport, which one would you choose? Would it be for the love of the game or the potential for fame and fortune?
4. Do you think athletes are overpaid, or do they deserve their wealth and fame? Why?
5. Do you think fame or fortune brings more happiness? Why?

BEFORE YOU READ

Read the statements. Check (✓) whether you agree or disagree with each statement. Discuss your answers with a partner.

	Strongly disagree	Disagree somewhat	Agree somewhat	Strongly agree
1. Children and teenagers should be encouraged to play sports regularly.				
2. Parents should invest in sports equipment and training for their children.				
3. Sports scholarships are a great way to pay for college.				
4. Professional athletes are good role models for kids.				
5. Athletes deserve the high salaries they get.				

VOCABULARY PREVIEW

1 Read the sentences. Circle the words closest in meaning to the words in bold.

1. Young people who **resolve** to become sports stars start training at a young age.
   a. dare   b. expect   c. decide

2. The **route** to success requires hard work and commitment.
   a. method   b. road   c. dream

3. The amount that parents spend on youth sports sometimes **exceeds** $12,000 a year.
   a. is equal to   b. is greater than   c. is close to

4. Even after young athletes have reached **adulthood**, it can take them years to start making money.
   a. responsibility   b. maturity   c. university

5. The salaries of athletes who get **drafted** by major sports teams are enormous.
   a. recruited   b. rejected   c. awarded

6. Football players in the NFL get paid a minimum of $660,000 **annually**.
   a. monthly   b. regularly   c. yearly

7. Many sports fans argue that the risk of **injury** justifies athletes' high salaries.
   a. victory   b. damage   c. failure

8. Athletes who have been injured can find themselves **physically** unable to do other work.
   a. completely   b. rarely   c. bodily

2 Match the words in bold in section 1 above to their definitions below.

________ : the part of someone's life when they are an adult

________ : once a year; each year

________ : to select for some purpose

________ : to be greater than or superior to

________ : hurt, damage, or loss

________ : in a physical manner; in respect to the body

________ : to reach a firm decision about

________ : an established or selected course of travel or action

FOR FAME AND FORTUNE?

Track 14

1. **Reading Skill: Setting a Purpose for Reading**
   Set a goal before reading, such as reading for enjoyment, learning technical information, seeing a new point of view, or learning about a subject.

2. **Critical-Thinking Skill: Detecting the Author's Purpose**
   Authors write for many reasons: to inform, persuade, entertain, etc. Knowing the author's purpose helps you think critically about the reading.

Growing up, many children and teenagers dream of becoming sports stars. They are drawn not only to the fame but also to the fortune that goes along with it, as they see their favorite football players or basketball stars on TV driving the latest cars and living in the most magnificent houses. Therefore, many young people are willing to spend both time and their parents' money chasing a career in sports. But what are the chances of sports success? And once an up-and-coming young athlete has attained pro status, how much financial reward is really going to come their way?

For those young people who resolve to achieve sports **stardom**[1], the investment starts early. The route to success requires young athletes to train daily and follow a healthy diet. This often means having to turn down invitations to parties and trips to fast-food restaurants with friends, so many **sacrifice**[2] their social lives completely. Such sporting **aspirations**[3] can also be very expensive. According to a recent report in *USA Today*, twenty percent of US families have a youth sports budget exceeding $12,000 a year per child. Spending includes buying expensive equipment, covering travel expenses, and paying for sports camps. And the costs don't stop when a child reaches adulthood. Many suffer from "forced amateurism," in which sports leagues in the US, in practice, force young people to go to college before they can go pro and start getting paid. Although many of these promising young athletes receive college **scholarships**[4] based on

1	**stardom**	*n.*	the quality of being famous, especially for being a singer, actor, sportsperson, etc.
2	**sacrifice**	*v.*	to give up (something that you want to keep), especially in order to get or do something else or to help someone
3	**aspiration**	*n.*	something that a person wants very much to achieve
4	**scholarship**	*n.*	a grant or payment to support a student's education

their abilities, many of their day-to-day expenses fall on their families.

Even those that make it through college on a sports scholarship often find they have a rough road ahead. For example, the National Collegiate Athletic Association (NCAA), an organization that helps facilitate scholarships, has over 450,000 athletes. Of these, only around 4,000 will ever become professional players in the four major US sports leagues: the NFL, NBA, MLB, and NHL. For those that do get drafted, the yearly salary is, of course, huge. Hockey players in the NHL get a minimum of $750,000 annually, while football players in the NFL make at least $660,000. But considering that an average athletic career lasts just five years, those numbers don't seem so unreasonable. Many athletes find themselves out of work completely once they retire, and this issue can be compounded by injury and a lack of experience in other areas. Retired pros may find themselves either physically unable or lacking the skills necessary to go into other lines of work.

The financial risk associated with pursuing a professional sports career is more **notable**[5] in sports such as track and field, swimming, and gymnastics. Many of these athletes rely on prize money from competitions to make a living. Such prizes can be generous; for example, competitors in the TYR Pro Swim Series can expect to receive $1,500 for each race they win, while second- and third-place finishers can win $1,000 and $500, **respectively**[6]. However, a long gap between wins can leave athletes financially unstable. This is a particular problem when events are canceled unexpectedly, as was the case during the early stages of the COVID-19 pandemic. Many athletes found themselves without a way to earn money and, as they were **classified**[7] as self-employed, received little support from the government. Sarah Hirshland, CEO of the US Olympic and Paralympic Committee, called these athletes "classic gig workers" because, while their work was potentially **lucrative**[8] during good times, it left athletes financially vulnerable during bad times.

For the vast majority who don't find success in professional sports, the risks are even higher. Many young people who have spent their years at school and university tirelessly training will have had little time left for their studies. This can leave them underqualified for the world of work they will one day find themselves in.

Sports can certainly be great for individuals, allowing them to test their limits and win applause for brilliant performances. And for those looking to become sports stars, it seems clear that this should be the driving force, not profit.

5	**notable**	*adj.*	worth noticing
6	**respectively**	*adv.*	in the order given
7	**classify**	*v.*	to consider (someone or something) as belonging to a particular group
8	**lucrative**	*adj.*	producing money or wealth

COMPREHENSION CHECK-UPS

1. **According to paragraph 1, which is true about many young people?**
   a. They believe that popularity is more important than wealth.
   b. They are influenced by the portrayal of sports stars in the media.
   c. They understand how difficult it is to become a professional athlete.
   d. They are pressured to take part in sports by their parents.

2. **According to paragraph 2, which of the following is NOT true?**
   a. Twenty percent of US families spend $20,000 a year on sports-related expenses.
   b. Sports scholarships help many young athletes pay for college tuition.
   c. Many young athletes give up opportunities to socialize in order to train.
   d. Top athletes are offered professional contracts when they reach eighteen.

3. **Which statement best restates the sentence, "Many suffer from "forced amateurism," in which sports leagues in the US, in practice, force young people to go to college before they can go pro and start getting paid." from paragraph 2?**
   a. US sports leagues force young athletes to complete college in order to go pro.
   b. Pro US sports leagues often use college facilities to practice before games.
   c. Pro sports teams often pay young athletes a salary while they attend college.
   d. Amateur athletes in the US push sports teams to hire them at a younger age.

4. **In paragraph 2, why does the author mention the *USA Today* report?**
   a. To explain why there are fewer aspiring athletes
   b. To encourage parents to invest more in youth athletics
   c. To compare the experiences between high- and low-income families
   d. To inform readers about the financial difficulties that athletics can cause families

5. **According to paragraph 3, what problem do NCAA athletes face?**
   a. Even those that get drafted as professionals are paid poorly.
   b. They have to pay for their own college tuition and living expenses.
   c. Less than one percent will get the chance to play for top US teams.
   d. They are required to gain additional work skills while training.

6. Read paragraph 3. Why does the writer believe that high salaries for football and hockey players are reasonable?

____

____

7. According to paragraph 4, which of the following is NOT true?

a. Swimmers and gymnasts face more financial risk than footballers.
b. Some believe that athletes are in a position similar to gig workers.
c. Athletes usually receive government support between competitions.
d. Taking part in athletic competitions can be profitable for the winners.

8. According to paragraph 5, which is true about young athletes who fail to go pro?

a. They risk earning less later in life.
b. They earn more in the long run.
c. They are likely to return to college.
d. They often find non-player roles with big sports teams.

9. Read paragraph 5. Why are young athletes who are unable to go pro at high risk financially?

____

____

10. What can be inferred from paragraphs 5 and 6?

a. Young people looking for financial security should not aim to become sports stars.
b. For many people, a career in sports is the quickest and easiest way to become rich.
c. A passion for sports is not a good enough reason to pursue an athletic career.
d. Many people pursue a sports career because they are not academically talented.

MAPPING IDEAS

Find the correct main idea and three supporting points. Then match them to the graphic organizer.

FOR FAME AND FORTUNE?		
	MAIN IDEA / THESIS	
	1. ________	
POINT 1	POINT 2	POINT 3
2. ________	3. ________	4. ________

a. Although athletes in the top US sports leagues get high salaries, they have short careers and may find themselves unemployed after retirement.
b. The Olympic and Paralympic Committee gives out generous monetary prizes for training and support when athletes are injured.
c. Young athletes and their families sacrifice their social lives and financial security for a chance of getting drafted by a top team.
d. Those young athletes who do not get professional contracts may find themselves unqualified for other types of work.
e. Many young people are drawn to the idea of being sports stars, but the reality is unlikely to live up to their expectations.
f. A sports scholarship from the NCAA more or less guarantees that a young athlete gets a place in a top professional team.

VOCABULARY REVIEW

Fill in the blanks with the correct words from the box. Change the form if needed.

injury	**aspiration**	**exceed**	**resolve**
adulthood	**route**	**lucrative**	**draft**

1. Every year, Sara ________ to make positive changes in her life on January 1.
2. During the COVID-19 pandemic, businesses that delivered goods to peoples' homes became very ________.
3. Mountain climbing, bull running, and hang gliding are dangerous and have high rates of ________.
4. I took the wrong ________ to my new workplace and ended up being half an hour late.
5. ________ brings not only new freedoms but also new responsibilities.
6. Some countries find it necessary to ________ citizens into the military.
7. Many people find that their ________ and desires change as they get older.
8. Drivers who ________ the speed limit in this city must pay a fine of at least $50.

CRITICAL-THINKING SKILL

Detecting the Author's Purpose

Authors write for many reasons. Common reasons include to entertain, to inform, to explain, to teach, to persuade, and to compare and contrast. Authors can also have more than one purpose.

Read the excerpts. Evaluate them with a partner and answer the questions.

1

For those young people who resolve to achieve sports stardom, the investment starts early. The route to success requires young athletes to train daily and follow a healthy diet. This often means having to turn down invitations to parties and trips to fast-food restaurants with friends, so many sacrifice their social lives completely. Such sporting aspirations can also be very expensive. According to a recent report in *USA Today*, twenty percent of US families have a youth sports budget exceeding $12,000 a year per child. Spending includes buying expensive equipment, covering travel expenses, and paying for sports camps.

PURPOSE Circle the purpose. Then underline the sentence that most clearly illustrates the purpose.

a. To entertain b. To compare and contrast c. To persuade d. To inform

SUMMARIZE Write a short summary of the author's purpose.

____

2

For the vast majority who don't find success in professional sports, the risks are even higher. Many young people who have spent their years at school and university tirelessly training will have had little time left for their studies. This can leave them underqualified for the world of work they will one day find themselves in.

PURPOSE Circle the purpose. Then underline the sentence that most clearly illustrates the purpose.

a. To entertain b. To compare and contrast c. To persuade d. To inform

SUMMARIZE Write a short summary of the author's purpose.

____

IDEAS IN DISCUSSION

1. What challenges do young athletes face when trying to go pro?

2. Do you know anyone who has tried to become a professional athlete? What was their experience like?

3. When choosing a career, do you think passion or financial security is more important? Explain your answer.

4. Do you think most athletes are driven more by a passion for their sport or the pursuit of fame and fortune? Why?

5. How has social media changed the way athletes achieve and manage fame and fortune?

IDEAS IN WRITING

Opinion Writing

1. Write a paragraph about whether the risks are worth the rewards for young athletes.

2. Should athletes be role models, or is their responsibility solely to their sport? Explain your stance.

Reflective Writing

3. Write about an athlete who inspires you. Do you admire them more for their fame, fortune, or contributions to their sport?

Inspirational Writing

4. Explore how an athlete can use their fame and fortune to give back to their community.

5. Describe how an underdog athlete rose to fame and fortune against all odds. What lessons can others learn from their journey?

CAREER

UNIT 8-1 What Do Gen Z Workers Want?

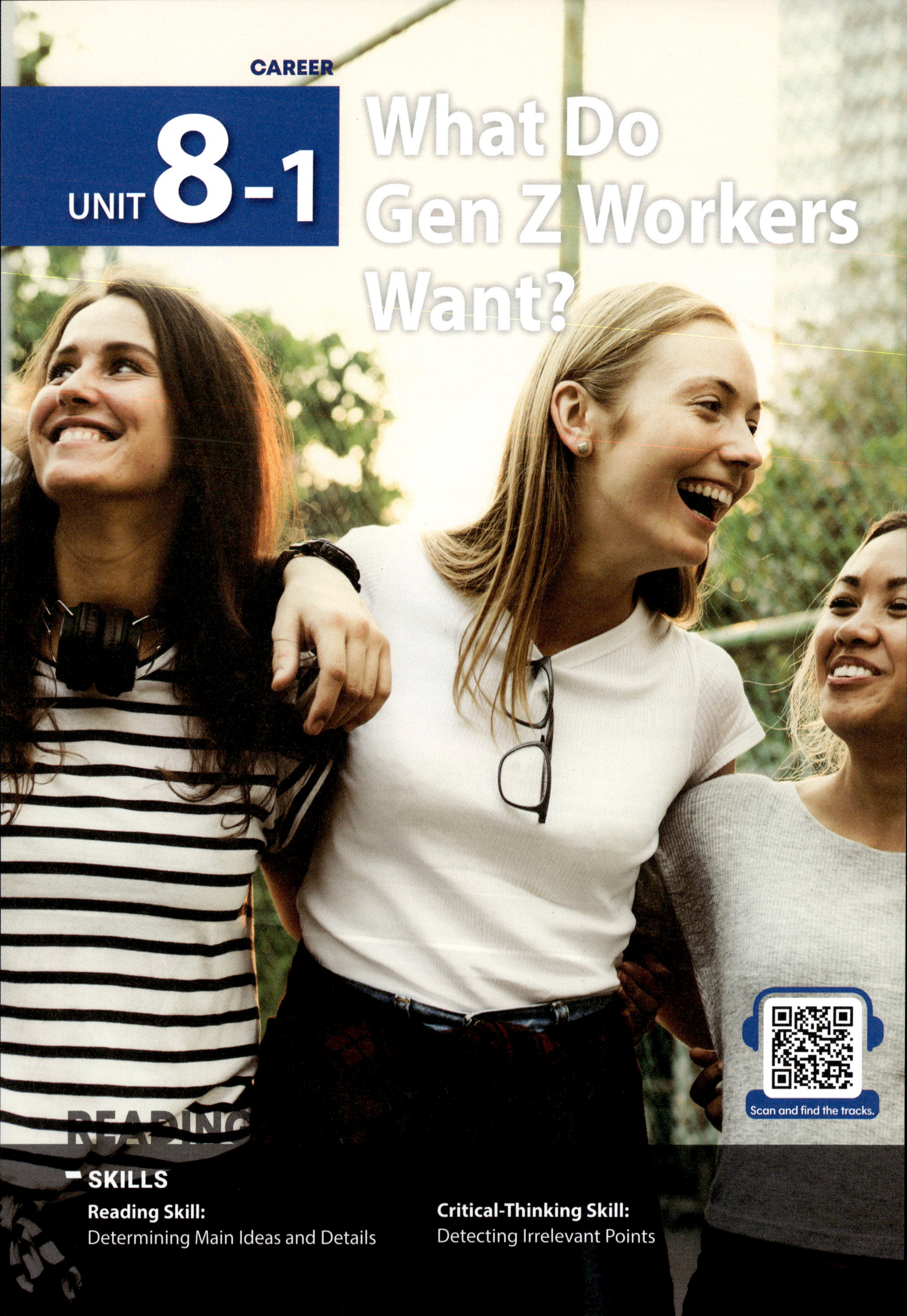

Scan and find the tracks.

READING

SKILLS

Reading Skill:
Determining Main Ideas and Details

Critical-Thinking Skill:
Detecting Irrelevant Points

WARM-UP QUESTIONS

1. What job would you like to do in the future?
2. What makes this job seem appealing?
3. What do you think is the most important factor in choosing a job: salary, work-life balance, or personal fulfillment?
4. What would you prioritize in your first job: high pay, opportunities for growth, or a supportive work culture?
5. What do you think is more important for Gen Z workers: job flexibility or job security?

BEFORE YOU READ

Read the statements. Check (✓) whether you agree or disagree with each statement. Discuss your answers with a partner.

	Strongly disagree	Disagree somewhat	Agree somewhat	Strongly agree
1. Companies should give employees learning opportunities and help with their education.				
2. Companies should offer work-from-home options.				
3. Companies should hire people from all backgrounds and treat them equally.				
4. Companies should make work fun and rewarding.				
5. Companies should prioritize paying high wages over other benefits.				

VOCABULARY PREVIEW

1 Read the sentences. Circle the words closest in meaning to the words in bold.

1. A **financially** dependable job is important to many Gen Zers.
   a. socially b. permanently c. economically

2. COVID-19 had a **disproportionate** impact on young people's lives.
   a. unequal b. unrealistic c. unbelievable

3. The **circumstances** of COVID-19, the economy, and climate change worried many.
   a. symbols b. conditions c. sights

4. Older people liked working from home; **conversely**, younger people did not.
   a. on the other hand b. later on c. at the same time

5. Gen Zers have started to **appreciate** having an obvious divide between work and leisure time.
   a. realize b. demand c. enjoy

6. Many Gen Zers want to expand on the **investment** they made in their education.
   a. extension b. exception c. expense

7. Companies that have **targeted** social projects are popular with young workers.
   a. approached b. prioritized c. purchased

8. The company has a five-point policy that includes supporting **community** trade.
   a. local b. common c. territorial

2 Match the words in section 1 above to their definitions below.

________ : to understand the worth or importance of something or someone

________ : a condition or fact that affects a situation

________ : the people with common interests living in a particular area

________ : in an opposite way

________ : too large or too small in comparison to something else, or not deserving of its importance or influence

________ : in a way that relates to money or how money is managed

________ : the money, effort, or time, etc. put into something to make a profit or get an advantage

________ : to direct one's action at a certain person, group, or issue

WHAT DO GEN Z WORKERS WANT?

Track 15

1. Reading Skill: Determining Main Ideas and Details
The topic sentence of each paragraph will state its main idea. Topic sentences are supported by details, which may include facts, statistics, expert opinions, observations, etc.

2. Critical-Thinking Skill: Detecting Irrelevant Points
Writers sometimes use irrelevant points to confuse readers, take attention away from the main topic, or make an argument seem stronger than it really is. Read carefully to avoid being tricked by irrelevant information.

Over the past twenty years, much has been written about what Millennials (those born between 1981 and 1996) expect from employment. In contrast to the generations that preceded them, they wanted fun, flexible, easy-going jobs and expected to be able to travel. They didn't live to work, or so the saying went; instead, they worked to live. Today, those born after 1996 are entering the world of work, and Gen Zers, as they are known, have different expectations again—but why?

First, Gen Zers' educational backgrounds may make a steadier, more traditional job desirable. By most measures, they are the best-educated generation that the planet has ever produced, but this has come at a great financial cost. University is now more expensive—and more essential—than ever before. Between 2010 and 2020, the average cost of **undergraduate tuition**[1] in the US almost doubled. To fund this, in 2020, the average student borrowed $30,030. Thus, Gen Zers' focus is less likely to be on **perks**[2] than on finding a financially secure job, since most have finished university in debt.

Another factor affecting Gen Z's expectations could be the COVID-19 pandemic, which had a disproportionate effect on younger workers. According to the Pew Research Center, half of Gen Zers either experienced a job loss themselves or had a family member who did. Considering these worrying circumstances, along with the ongoing impact of the 2008 financial crisis and the threat of climate change, it's no wonder that young people have become anxious about their futures. So

1 **undergraduate tuition** *n.* the money students pay for a (usually) four-year degree qualification at university
2 **perk** *n.* an extra advantage, other than a payment

once again, instead of flexibility, many Gen Zers found themselves seeking stability.

With time, other trends may also be reversed. During the pandemic, many older workers appreciated the break from office life and felt that working from home might be "the future." Conversely, and perhaps surprisingly, younger people did not feel the same. In one survey, just thirty-four percent of older workers complained about working from home, whereas forty-seven percent of Gen Zers did, often citing its negative effect on their mental health. In part, this may be because they typically have smaller, less comfortable homes or still live with their parents. In addition, some Gen Zers suspect that working flexibly between the home and office actually means an increased workload overall.

Young workers appreciate the clear distinction between home and work that a nine-to-five job provides. They rightly expect to be both trained and listened to by their bosses and know that this happens best face-to-face: research shows that members of this generation value personal development above all. Expanding on the initial investment of their educations, job seekers now put opportunities for continued learning and development at the top of their lists of requirements. Many look for programs like that of US communications company AT&T, which recently opened its own "university" for staff at its headquarters, which keeps its employees informed about the latest technologies.

Another change in employment expectations is an increased interest in social responsibility. When job-hunting, social and environmental considerations are now a bigger priority than ever before, with eighty-five percent of Gen Z job seekers saying that "serving a purpose and leaving a positive **legacy**[3] for future generations" was important to them. Young people seek employment at companies like The Body Shop, which has targeted environmental sustainability and socially beneficial projects with its five-point policy: "support community trade, defend human rights, stand against animal testing, **activate**[4] self-esteem, and protect our planet." Furthermore, as the most ethnically diverse generation ever, Gen Zers also expect companies to have **inclusive**[5] employment policies which reflect the world outside. As well as being ethically sound, these kinds of policies define a company as dynamic, progressive, and "going places," making it a safe economic **bet**[6] for the future.

Today, some employment experts have already moved on to consider the needs of Generation Alpha (children born after 2010), but this is probably a **fool's errand**[7]. Gen Z has shown us that unpredictable worldwide factors can quickly reverse trends and create new needs. Like Millennials, Gen Zers expect to be paid well for their work; however, the main perks they require are no longer flexibility and freedom but stability and ethics.

3	**legacy**	*n.*	something handed down from the past or that comes from someone in the past
4	**activate**	*v.*	to cause something to start
5	**inclusive**	*adj.*	trying to include different types of people and treat them all equally
6	**bet**	*n.*	something, usually an amount of money, wagered on the outcome of an event
7	**fool's errand**	*idiom.*	an effort that is unlikely to be successful

COMPREHENSION CHECK-UPS

1. According to paragraph 1, which of the following did Millennials NOT expect from their workplace?
   a. To have a stable job
   b. To be able to travel
   c. To have a flexible job
   d. To enjoy their job

2. In paragraph 1, why does the author write, "They didn't live to work"?
   a. To suggest that Millennials were lazier than those that followed them
   b. To explain that Gen Zers don't feel the same about work as Millennials do
   c. To tell us that work was not the number-one priority for Millennials
   d. To show how Millennials struggled to survive in jobs with long hours

3. According to paragraph 2, which is true about Gen Zers?
   a. They are not very interested in traditional jobs.
   b. They value education less than people did in the past.
   c. They paid more for college than previous generations.
   d. They prioritize perks when looking for employment.

4. Read paragraph 2. Write the sentence that could be deleted without affecting the meaning of the paragraph.

   ____

   ____

5. Which statement best restates the sentence, "Considering these worrying circumstances, along with the ongoing impact of the 2008 financial crisis and the threat of climate change, it's no wonder that young people have become anxious about their futures." from paragraph 3?
   a. Global events made companies less likely to hire young people.
   b. A series of incredible phenomena have left young people confused.
   c. One group of young people predicted a chain of terrible world events.
   d. Members of Gen Z feel anxious because of several negative world events.

6. Read paragraph 3. Why does the author cite the Pew Research Center?

____

____

7. According to paragraph 4, which was NOT a factor in Gen Zers wanting to return to the office?

a. They were worried about being overlooked in favor of older workers.

b. They suspected that they would have to work more if working from home.

c. They often had less comfortable work conditions at home.

d. They felt that working from home hurt their mental health.

8. According to paragraph 5, what is most important to Gen Z workers?

a. Having separate personal and professional lives

b. Communicating with senior staff at their companies

c. Knowing they have access to educational opportunities

d. Working directly alongside other colleagues

9. According to paragraph 6, what appeals to Gen Zers about companies like The Body Shop?

a. Diversity

b. Ethnicity

c. Flexibility

d. Ethics

10. What can be inferred from paragraph 6?

a. Companies that do not embrace inclusivity will be at a disadvantage.

b. Many companies wrongly believe that diversity is too progressive.

c. Gen Zers choose companies with the best economic prospects.

d. Companies adopt ethical practices to attract the best workers.

MAPPING IDEAS

Find the correct main idea and three supporting points. Then match them to the graphic organizer.

WHAT DO GEN Z WORKERS WANT?		
MAIN IDEA / THESIS		
1. ______		
POINT 1	POINT 2	POINT 3
2. ______	3. ______	4. ______

a. Gen Z workers prefer working in offices because they believe remote and flexible hours result in more working time.
b. Gen Z workers have different expectations of the ideal workplace than previous generations.
c. Gen Z workers do not prefer on-the-job training and rather increase their time learning at school.
d. Because of difficult living conditions, Gen Z workers prefer to work at companies with flexibility and job perks.
e. Due to large debt levels, Gen Z workers prefer jobs that provide financial stability over perks.
f. More than any previous generation, Gen Z workers prefer working at environmentally and socially conscious companies.

VOCABULARY REVIEW

Fill in the blanks with the correct words from the box. Change the form if needed.

financially	disproportionate	circumstance	appreciate
investment	target	community	legacy

1. The sportswear company ______ younger customers with its latest ad campaign.
2. Dan found himself in a difficult ______ when his car broke down in the snow.
3. The president's ______ is impressive; over eight years, she built many schools, homes, and hospitals.
4. There's a(n) ______ park nearby where kids can play with others in the neighborhood.
5. Mr. Schmidt lives alone, so he really ______ receiving visitors.
6. Global warming is mainly caused by developed nations but is set to have a(n) ______ effect on poorer ones.
7. Pedro is ______ comfortable—he has a nice home and drives a new car.
8. I've had this winter coat for ten years, so while it cost a lot, it was a good ______.

CRITICAL-THINKING SKILL

Detecting Irrelevant Points

Writers sometimes use irrelevant points to confuse readers, take attention away from the main topic, or make an argument seem stronger than it really is. Careful readers can distinguish points that are related to the argument and those that are not. By ignoring irrelevant points, readers can avoid being distracted and focus on evaluating the writer's main argument. For example:

(1) Violent crime is common in areas where people have easy access to guns.

(2) The US has more guns per person than any other nation.

(3) Therefore, the government should make it more difficult for people to buy guns.

Statement 2 is related to the topic; however, the conclusion (statement 3) doesn't follow from it.

1 Read the excerpt. Evaluate it with a partner and complete the activities.

MAIN IDEA *The COVID-19 pandemic has had a noticeable effect on what Gen Zers look for in a job.*

(1) Eight in ten recent college graduates say that the experience gave them greater confidence in their ability to adapt and overcome obstacles. This quality is sure to be helpful in their search for a dream job. **(2)** Members of this generation also report that the worldwide public-health crisis has made them more empathetic and eager to help others. As a result, forty-five percent are considering careers in healthcare or related scientific fields.

Is part (1) relevant to the main idea of the paragraph? ☐ Yes ☐ No

Is part (2) relevant to the main idea of the paragraph? ☐ Yes ☐ No

2 Summarize the excerpt.

____

____

____

IDEAS IN DISCUSSION

1. Are you confident that higher education is a good investment? Why or why not?

2. How important is it to you for your future company to be ethical?

3. What do you want most from your future job?

4. How do Gen Z's work preferences differ from Millennials or Gen X? Are these differences significant or overstated?

5. Do you think Gen Z workers are more likely to avoid companies that don't align with their personal values?

IDEAS IN WRITING

Hypothetical and Future-Focused Writing

1. Write a paragraph outlining your hopes for your future job. Which do they match more, the desires of Millennials or those of Gen Zers? (From the textbook)

Reflective Writing

2. What do you think Gen Z workers value most in a job, and why? Reflect on how these values align or differ from your own priorities.
3. How has growing up with technology influenced the workplace expectations of Gen Z?

Analytical Writing

4. Discuss the importance of diversity and inclusion in the workplace for Gen Z workers. Why do these values matter to them?

Exploratory Writing

5. Explore how social media influences Gen Z's perception of career success and workplace culture.

CAREER

UNIT 8-2 Kicking the Nine-to-Five

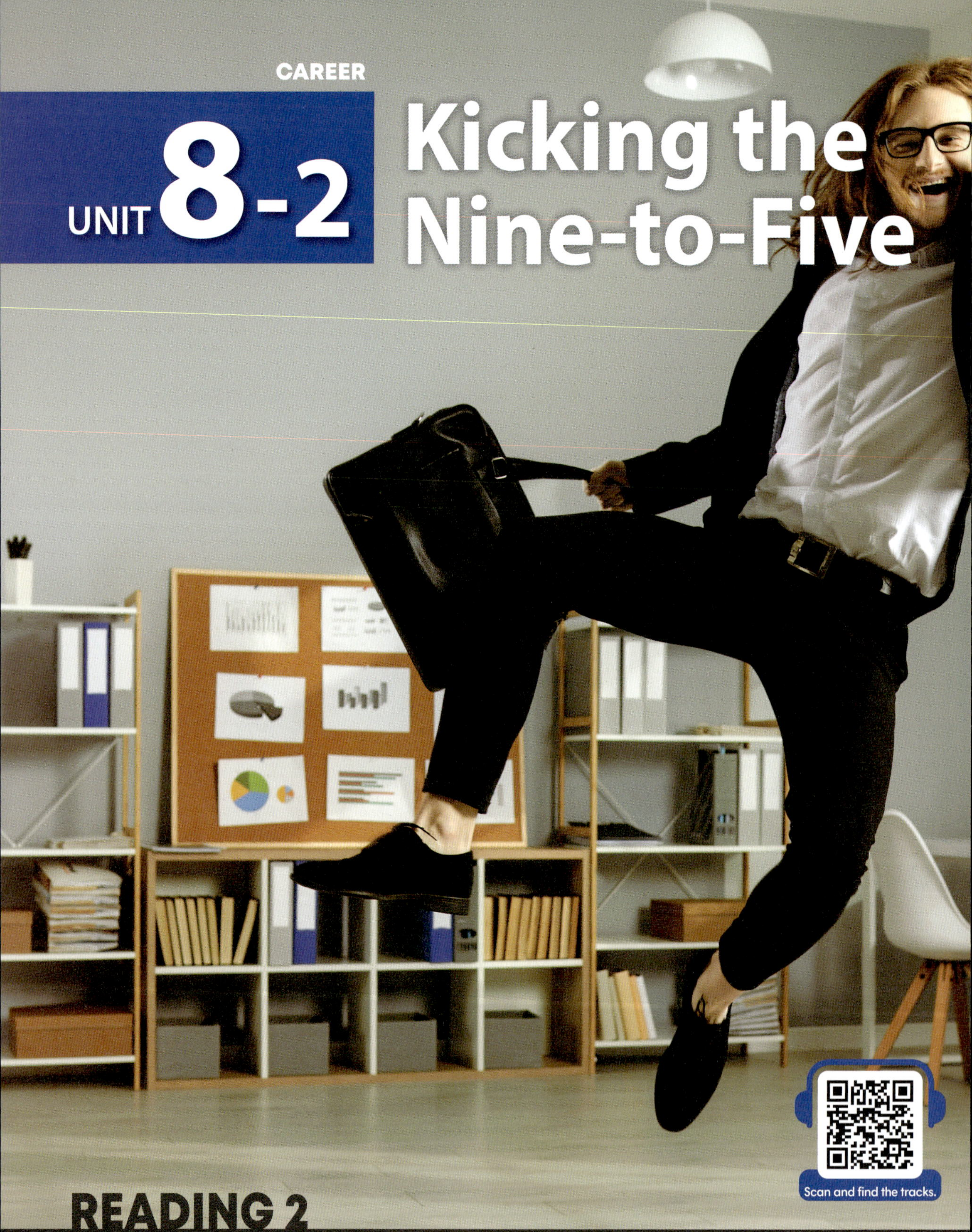

Scan and find the tracks.

READING 2

SKILLS

Reading Skill:
Determining Main Ideas and Details

Critical-Thinking Skill:
Detecting Persuasive Language

WARM-UP QUESTIONS

1. If you could choose, what hours of the day would you like to work?
2. What are some reasons for wanting to work irregular hours?
3. What do you think would be the biggest challenge in leaving a nine-to-five job?
4. What's one skill or talent you have that could help you start something outside the traditional workplace?
5. What's a success story you've heard about someone leaving the nine-to-five that inspires you?

BEFORE YOU READ

Rank the statements from 1 (most true about you) to 6 (least true about you). Discuss your rankings with a partner.

__________ I concentrate better at night.

__________ I am most productive in the morning.

__________ I tend to grow tired in the afternoon.

__________ I like to stay up late most nights.

__________ I am happy to wake up early every day.

__________ I think nine-to-five is the best working schedule.

VOCABULARY PREVIEW

1 Read the sentences. Circle the words closest in meaning to the words in bold.

1. Our business was **founded** with the idea that staff would work traditional office hours.
   a. utilized　b. developed　c. established

2. The people I started the business with are most **energetic** in the morning.
   a. accurate　b. lively　c. stylish

3. After a while, we questioned our **assumptions** about traditional working hours.
   a. beliefs　b. reservations　c. intentions

4. The traditional workday has been around for one hundred years, which is why people **justify** keeping it.
   a. confirm　b. rationalize　c. verify

5. In the 1920s, governments started **specifying** the forty-hour workweek in labor laws.
   a. interpreting　b. referencing　c. defining

6. People's bodily rhythms differ and **trigger** fatigue at different times of the day.
   a. predict　b. prompt　c. prepare

7. Our business instituted a system **whereby** 11:00 a.m. to 3:00 p.m. were required working hours.
   a. as a result　b. by the way　c. by which

8. We got rid of this because the **qualitative** aspects of work were more important than the quantitative ones.
   a. subjective　b. statistical　c. collective

2 Match the words in section 1 above to their definitions below.

________ : a fact or statement taken for granted

________ : having or involving a lot of energy

________ : to bring something into existence

________ : to give or to be a good reason for

________ : relating to how good or bad something is

________ : to name or state explicitly or in particular

________ : to initiate or set something off

________ : by, through, or in accordance with which

KICKING THE NINE-TO-FIVE

Track 16

1. **Reading Skill: Determining Main Ideas and Details**
   The topic sentence of each paragraph will state its main idea. Topic sentences are supported by details, which may include facts, statistics, expert opinions, observations, etc.

2. **Critical-Thinking Skill: Detecting Persuasive Language**
   Writers use emotional language to persuade readers to feel a certain way about a topic. Readers should be aware of emotional language that affects their reasoning.

When we founded our company, my partners and I assumed that we'd keep regular office hours. I mean, every other job any of us have ever had was a nine-to-five, so why should ours be any different? Well, the problem was that, like many developers, I'm a **night owl**[1], so I don't get going until about noon. Also, I'm at my most productive between 8:00 p.m. and midnight. My co-founders are the opposite. They're the most energetic first thing in the morning, and by mid-afternoon, they're ready to crash. We all struggled for the first three months—I could hardly stay awake at morning meetings, and they were exhausted from my late-night phone calls.

Our **fledgling**[2] start-up's problems made us examine our assumptions about our working hours, and a quick look at history reveals just how outdated our modern standard is. The current workday emerged almost a hundred years ago: a different era with different demands and needs. If there were good reasons for it a hundred years ago—reasons that still apply today—then perhaps we could justify maintaining it.

Well, the fact is that there were never compelling reasons for adopting the forty-hour workweek. During the 1920s, the Industrial Revolution was in full swing, and factories typically ran twenty-four hours a day, with workers doing ten- to sixteen-hour shifts. Then Ford Motor Company founder Henry Ford established a five-day, forty-hour workweek while paying the same wages. Ford later explained that he had made the change to give workers more time to shop—

1	**night owl**	*n.*	a person who likes to stay up late
2	**fledgling**	*adj.*	newly formed and still developing

specifically, to buy his cars. Regardless of the motivation, other manufacturers **followed suit**[3], and gradually, governments began specifying the forty-hour workweek as part of labor law.

A uniform work schedule made some sense at the time because the office was the **locus**[4] of work, and workers had to be available during work hours to collaborate in person. However, in the era of laptops, cell phones, and **ubiquitous**[5] wireless connectivity, do arguments for this model continue to carry any weight?

The conventional workday is ideal for one type of person in particular: the **early bird**[6]. Research shows that genetic factors determine the length of a person's circadian cycle: the biological signals that influence the body's rise and fall in energy levels and trigger drowsiness, wakefulness, hunger, etc. According to Katherine Sharkey, a professor at Brown University, this cycle determines whether someone is an early bird or a night owl. If your cycle is a bit shorter, you're likely an early bird, and the nine-to-five routine suits you perfectly. When you come to work in the morning, you're all **fired up**[7] and ready to go, but by the end of the day, you are **running on empty**[8].

But what if you are more productive later in the day or at night, like a **sizable**[9] proportion of the population? The nine-to-five routine forces night owls to be productive when their **alertness**[10] and energy level are naturally at their lowest. As a result, night owls typically get a reputation for being lazy or unmotivated. This assessment is unfair, given that they are merely victims of their own wake-sleep cycle, which they are more or less incapable of changing.

Several steps led to our company's eventual break from the traditional nine-to-five schedule. Originally, we adopted a "flextime" system whereby everyone had to be at the office between 11:00 a.m. and 3:00 p.m.; beyond that, they could just come and go as they liked, provided they worked a full eight hours a day. However, flextime was abandoned after a few months because the quantitative measure of how many hours someone worked wasn't as important to us as the qualitative aspect. We wanted beautiful, creative products and brilliant solutions to problems, and we found we got more of those out of our team when we let them set their own schedules.

On the surface, having no set working hours might seem like a recipe for disaster, but for our company, it's been perfect. Since abandoning a set work schedule, we've seen improvements in our productivity, our health, and the overall quality of our lives. It's a decision we've never regretted, and it's one I would recommend to other business owners.

3	**follow suit**	*idiom*	to do the same as
4	**locus**	*n.*	a central place; a site where something happens
5	**ubiquitous**	*adj.*	found everywhere; very common
6	**early bird**	*n.*	a person who likes to get up early
7	**fired up**	*idiom*	excited about or impatient to do something
8	**running on empty**	*idiom*	out of energy or resources
9	**sizable**	*adj.*	fairly large
10	**alertness**	*n.*	the state of being mentally aware and able to think clearly

COMPREHENSION CHECK-UPS

1. According to paragraph 1, what problem did the business face?
   a. It didn't plan to operate within a traditional workday.
   b. Developers at other businesses worked different hours.
   c. Some staff wanted to work longer hours than others.
   d. Staff found they functioned best at different times of the day.

2. According to paragraph 3, why did Henry Ford favor a forty-hour workweek?
   a. He found he could reduce his expenses by paying staff lower wages.
   b. He needed staff to keep his factories running through the night.
   c. He wanted employees to have leisure time to buy his cars.
   d. He thought the government would punish him for overworking his staff.

3. Read the first sentence of paragraph 3. Do you think the author is for or against the forty-hour workweek?

   ____

   ____

4. In paragraph 3, why does the author use the phrase "in full swing"?
   a. To say that automakers employed energetic employees
   b. To explain that manufacturing was at its peak
   c. To suggest that many countries were starting to change
   d. To explain why cars were becoming more ubiquitous

5. Which statement best restates the sentence, "A uniform work schedule made some sense at the time because the office was the locus of work, and workers had to be available during work hours to collaborate in person." from paragraph 4?
   a. In the past, colleagues were often closer and more friendly to one another.
   b. Workers were once expected to have extreme loyalty to their employers.
   c. Historically, businesses trusted their staff less and monitored their work more.
   d. In those days, being in the office was the most practical way to work.

6. Read paragraph 4. Why might uniform work schedules no longer be appropriate?

____

____

7. According to paragraph 5, all of the following are true EXCEPT _______.

a. the standard workday is designed for those who wake early
b. circadian cycles are determined by the time we go to bed
c. people with shorter cycles are best suited to traditional working hours
d. our circadian cycles determine when we want to sleep, eat, and work

8. Which of the following is NOT stated about night owls in paragraph 6?

a. People often think they are not motivated.
b. They try harder than their early-bird colleagues.
c. Colleagues may unfairly assess their abilities.
d. They can't control the way their bodies work.

9. According to paragraph 7, what is the company's priority?

a. Product excellence
b. Employees' welfare
c. Work flexibility
d. Work-life balance

10. What can be inferred from paragraph 7?

a. Flextime was too revolutionary.
b. Workers demanded a flextime policy.
c. Early-bird employees hated flextime.
d. Flextime did not improve work quality.

MAPPING IDEAS

Find the correct main idea and three supporting points. Then match them to the graphic organizer.

KICKING THE NINE-TO-FIVE		
MAIN IDEA / THESIS		
1. ________		
POINT 1 - PARAGRAPH 3	POINT 2 - PARAGRAPH 5	POINT 3 - PARAGRAPH 7
2. ________	3. ________	4. ________

a. Now that we have the internet and cell phones, staff can work anywhere at any time.
b. The reasons for a forty-hour workweek address the demands and needs of companies in a different era.
c. The company changed its policy, allowing staff to choose which hours they worked.
d. The traditional nine-to-five workday is not necessarily the best fit for all people and industries.
e. Our bodies are genetically programmed to function best at certain times of the day.
f. Those who sleep later often find that their reputation at work can suffer.

VOCABULARY REVIEW

Fill in the blanks with the correct words from the box. Change the form if needed.

energetic	assumption	justify	specify
trigger	whereby	fledgling	ubiquitous

1. Our library has a strict system ________ users can only keep a book for three weeks.
2. For those with a wheat allergy, eating bread could ________ stomach complaints.
3. Students in US colleges usually study several subjects but ________ one as their major.
4. It is now highly successful, but in the early years, the ________ music magazine only sold a few copies.
5. When given sugar, children can suddenly become highly ________.
6. Only a few people had smartphones in the early 2000s, but today they're ________.
7. The student attempted to ________ his lateness, but his explanation was unconvincing.
8. It is not fair or useful to make ________ about someone based on their appearance.

CRITICAL-THINKING SKILL

Detecting Persuasive Language

Writers use emotional language to persuade readers to feel a certain way about a topic. However, the strength of an argument should stand on good reason and evidence. Readers need to be cautious and evaluate arguments fairly. Note how the following statement changes when the underlined words are removed.

Countless people are seriously maimed in traffic accidents. → People are hurt in traffic accidents.

Read the excerpts. Evaluate them with a partner and answer the questions.

1 Our fledgling start-up's problems made us examine our assumptions about our working hours, and a quick look at history reveals just how outdated our modern standard is. The current workday emerged almost a hundred years ago: a different era with different demands and needs. If there were good reasons for it a hundred years ago—reasons that still apply today—then perhaps we could justify maintaining it.

DETECTING LANGUAGE Underline any words or phrases that appeal to the reader's emotions.

PURPOSE Why does the author use this kind of language?

____

2 But what if you are more productive later in the day or at night, like a sizable proportion of the population? The nine-to-five routine forces night owls to be productive when their alertness and energy level are naturally at their lowest. As a result, night owls typically get a reputation for being lazy or unmotivated. This assessment is unfair, given that they are merely victims of their own wake-sleep cycle, which they are more or less incapable of changing.

DETECTING LANGUAGE Underline any words or phrases that appeal to the reader's emotions.

PURPOSE Why does the author use this kind of language?

____

IDEAS IN DISCUSSION

1. Are you a night owl or an early bird?

2. Do you think it's unfair to make night owls start work or school early in the morning?

3. In general, do you prefer routines or not? Why?

4. What are the first steps someone should take if they want to transition out of a traditional nine-to-five job?

5. How has technology enabled or hindered the ability to escape the traditional workplace?

IDEAS IN WRITING

Opinion Writing

1. Write a paragraph about whether businesses should or should not have fixed working hours. (Based on the textbook reading)

2. Should schools and universities prepare students for alternative career paths instead of traditional jobs? Explain your position.

Analytical Writing

3. Explore the financial challenges of leaving a stable job and how people can prepare for such a transition.

4. Analyze the pros and cons of leaving a traditional job.

Creative Writing

5. Imagine the future of work: What would a world without traditional nine-to-five jobs look like?

SOCIOLOGY

UNIT 9-1 People over Profits

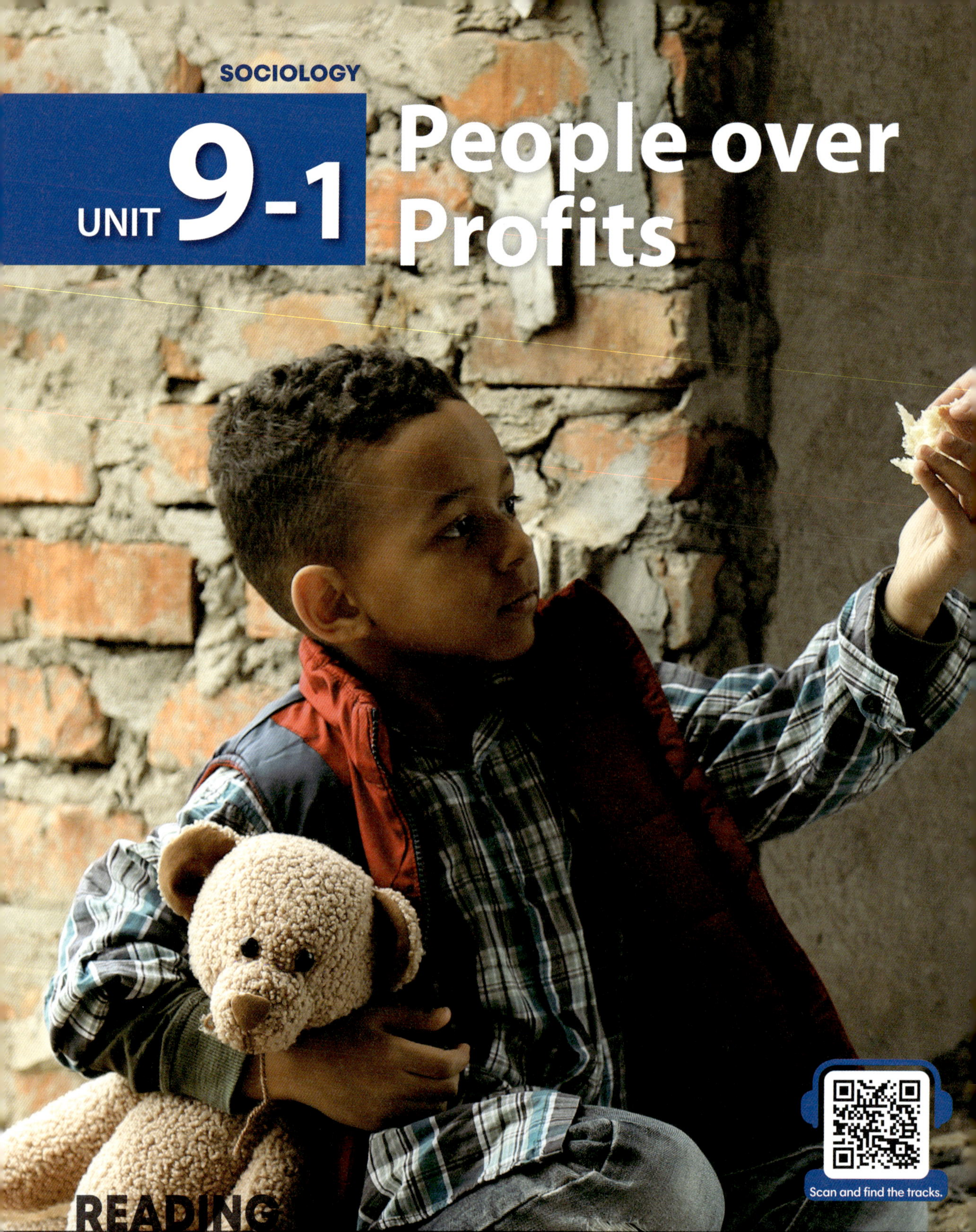

Scan and find the tracks.

READING

SKILLS

Reading Skill:
Determining Main Ideas and Details

Critical-Thinking Skill:
Detecting Persuasive Language

WARM-UP QUESTIONS

1. What are the main causes of homelessness and hunger in wealthy countries?
2. Do you think it's possible to end these problems completely? Why or why not?
3. Give some examples of welfare programs your government provides people in need and their families.
4. What is unemployment insurance for?
5. Have you ever heard of "universal basic income (UBI)"?

BEFORE YOU READ

Rank the statements from 1 (most agree with) to 6 (least agree with). Discuss your rankings with a partner.

_________ The government should protect the nation from outside threats.

_________ The government should make laws to protect people from bad employers.

_________ The government should maintain essential utilities such as electricity and water.

_________ The government should work to solve social problems like poverty and starvation.

_________ The government should work to solve economic problems like price inflation and unemployment.

_________ The government should create equal access to basic services like education and healthcare for all citizens.

VOCABULARY PREVIEW

1 Read the sentences. Circle the words closest in meaning to the words in bold.

1. It's the government's job to ensure safe **infrastructure** for the public.
   a. workplaces b. programs c. buildings

2. Governments use **regulations** to ensure safety at home, work, and in public.
   a. processes b. departments c. laws

3. Regular **inspections** of businesses are needed to ensure that they follow safety standards.
   a. examinations b. exercises c. reservations

4. Government programs such as **welfare** are used to ease the problems of low-income individuals.
   a. protection b. support c. information

5. A new economic **policy** could solve the problems of homelessness and poverty.
   a. program b. condition c. market

6. Countries can save money by **implementing** a universal basic income.
   a. improving b. starting c. judging

7. Taxes used to **fund** welfare programs could be used toward a universal basic income.
   a. adapt to b. pay for c. rely on

8. The cost of **administration** for welfare programs can be reduced with a universal basic income.
   a. budget b. schedule c. management

2 Match the words in section 1 above to their definitions below.

________ : the act or process of managing or dealing with a business activity

________ : to provide the money to pay for an event, activity, or organization

________ : to start using a plan or system

________ : the basic systems and services, such as transportation and power supplies, that a country or organization uses in order to work effectively

________ : the act of checking or testing something carefully against established standards

________ : a set of ideas or a plan of what to do that has been agreed to officially by a group of people, a business organization, a government, or a political party

________ : an official rule or the act of controlling something

________ : help given by the state to people who need it, especially because they do not have enough money

PEOPLE OVER PROFITS

Track 17

1. **Reading Skill: Determining Main Ideas and Details**
   The topic sentence of each paragraph will state its main idea. Topic sentences are supported by details, which may include facts, statistics, expert opinions, observations, etc.

2. **Critical-Thinking Skill: Detecting Persuasive Language**
   Writers use emotional language to persuade readers to feel a certain way about a topic. Readers should be aware of emotional language that affects their reasoning.

To create the conditions necessary for a productive society, the government should ensure some basic human safety and survival needs. For example, the government provides security through the military, police, and legal system. It also ensures safe housing, **workplaces**[1], and infrastructure through regulations, inspections, and other methods. However, when it comes to wealth, individuals are expected to take responsibility for themselves and their families. Unfortunately, even though many people work extremely hard to provide for their families, unexpected events can cause great financial trouble. Economic depressions, for example, leave millions struggling to support their families. Natural disasters have also destroyed many people's ability to make a living. Additionally, innovations such as **automated**[2] labor cause great shifts in the labor force and can suddenly leave many without a job.

What, then, should the government do to support people who are trying to be productive but have fallen on unfortunate times? How can governments address **socioeconomic**[3] problems such as homelessness, hunger, and unemployment? If these conditions are left unchecked, they can lead to **destitution**[4] for many individuals. If too many people are left destitute, the result may lead to other socioeconomic problems. These problems range from rising crime to **deflation**[5] and increasing class tension.

1 **workplace** *n.* the office, factory, etc. where people work
2 **automated** *adj.* done by a machine automatically or without needing to be controlled
3 **socioeconomic** *adj.* related to or involving the interaction of social and economic factors
4 **destitution** *n.* a state of being extremely poor
5 **deflation** *n.* a reduction of the supply of money in an economy, and therefore a reduction of economic activity

Nowadays, a combination of social safety net programs such as welfare and unemployment insurance, along with charities and non-profit organizations, work to ease these problems. These efforts are better than nothing. However, a growing number of people feel that welfare programs and charities don't do enough to resolve social problems. Recent census information from the US shows that one in ten Americans lives at or below the poverty line, even with existing social programs. In addition, government agencies in the US have estimated that homelessness affects anywhere between 600,000 and 1.5 million people. Clearly, something else is needed to help these people who have **slipped through the cracks**[6].

A relatively new economic policy idea called universal basic income (UBI) could address these issues. The basic idea of a UBI is that the government collects taxes and distributes enough money for each person, including children, to afford shelter and food every month. Citizens would receive this money **regardless of**[7] whether or not they work.

UBI supporters say that the policy could be a massive improvement to economic efficiency. Implementing UBI could save societies money by replacing other, more complicated welfare programs. The taxes currently used to fund those programs and their administration could be lowered. Furthermore, under a UBI, people enduring dull, miserable jobs would be free to find work or start businesses they actually like. This would make them more productive. Other social problems related to poverty, such as crime, would also be reduced. A lower crime rate would lead to a safer society that doesn't have to spend as much tax money on policing and prisons.

In addition, if regulations are placed on how and where a UBI is spent, it could protect local economies. UBI experiments in South Korea's Gyeonggi province have found that food sellers at local markets experienced increased sales, helping them maintain their businesses during challenging times. These sales increases were mainly due to a rule that made UBI funds usable only at registered local businesses. Citizens were not allowed to spend their UBI at stores owned by large corporations. This rule was added because bigger companies can weather economic challenges more easily.

As a nation grows increasingly **prosperous**[8], it seems clear that it should also change its policies to better protect life, liberty, and the pursuit of happiness. By ensuring basic human needs with a UBI, a government can not only help millions but also create the necessary conditions for continued growth and productivity.

6	**slip through the cracks**	*idiom*	to not be noticed or dealt with by a system; to not receive needed attention or help
7	**regardless of**	*ph. adv.*	despite; without being stopped or affected by something
8	**prosperous**	*adj.*	wealthy and successful

COMPREHENSION CHECK-UPS

1. According to paragraph 1, all of the following are mentioned as causes of poverty EXCEPT ________.
   a. natural disasters
   b. government regulations
   c. economic depressions
   d. innovations

2. Read paragraph 2. What might result from leaving too many people destitute?

   ____

   ____

3. According to paragraph 3, how many Americans are living at or below the poverty line?
   a. Ten percent
   b. 600,000
   c. 1.5 million
   d. Uncertain

4. In paragraph 4, what does the writer state about UBI?
   a. It does not involve payments to children.
   b. It will be paid for by charities.
   c. It is an old and familiar idea.
   d. It is intended for basic necessities.

5. Which statement best restates the sentence, "Citizens would receive this money regardless of whether or not they work." from paragraph 4?
   a. As long as citizens pay taxes, they can receive the money.
   b. Only taxpayers who are employed can get UBI.
   c. People would get UBI even if they do not have a job.
   d. If people get the money, then they don't have to work.

6. According to paragraph 5, what is a possible result of implementing UBI?

a. Improved economic efficiency
b. Improving working conditions
c. Removing regulations on new businesses
d. Making other welfare programs more efficient

7. What can be inferred from paragraph 5?

a. Happier people are more efficient at work.
b. The majority of people dislike their jobs.
c. Most welfare programs are run efficiently.
d. Current tax levels are probably too low.

8. According to paragraph 6, what determined how a person could spend their UBI in Gyeonggi province?

a. The product being purchased
b. The amount of the purchase
c. The size of the business
d. The income of the customer

9. In paragraph 6, why does the author mention food sellers in South Korea?

a. To illustrate the type of person who needs a UBI the most
b. To illustrate why welfare does not work well anymore
c. To illustrate how a UBI motivates people to work harder
d. To illustrate how a UBI could benefit local businesses

10. Read paragraph 6 and write the reason for Gyeonggi's rule regarding UBI spending.

____

____

MAPPING IDEAS

Find the correct main idea and three supporting points. Then match them to the graphic organizer.

PEOPLE OVER PROFITS		
MAIN IDEA / THESIS		
1. ______		
POINT 1	POINT 2	POINT 3
2. ______	3. ______	4. ______

a. Existing welfare programs are ineffective at dealing with socioeconomic problems.
b. A UBI is a good way to ensure a functional and productive society by providing for basic needs.
c. UBI requires additional taxpayer money for administration and management.
d. Automation will destroy jobs, so the government has to do something that will guarantee people an income.
e. Socioeconomic problems like poverty, homelessness, and joblessness could affect all citizens, so the government should find solutions to these problems.
f. A UBI boosts the local economy, makes people more productive, and reduces other social problems related to poverty.

VOCABULARY REVIEW

Fill in the blanks with the correct words from the box. Change the form if needed.

regulation	**fund**	**automated**	**welfare**
destitution	**inspection**	**implement**	**administration**

1. Many companies use ______ systems to deal with customer complaints.
2. The chief operating officer (COO) is in charge of the day-to-day ______ of a business.
3. The government created new ______ which will reduce unsafe environmental practices.
4. After losing his house and job, the man was left in a state of ______.
5. Investors are people who help ______ businesses by buying stocks.
6. The restaurant was closed after it failed a(n) ______ by the city health department.
7. Many people who live at or below the poverty line qualify for ______.
8. The company is ______ a program to help its employees gain new skills.

CRITICAL-THINKING SKILL

Detecting Persuasive Language

Writers use emotional language to persuade readers to feel a certain way about a topic. However, the strength of an argument should stand on good reason and evidence. Readers need to be cautious and evaluate arguments fairly. Note how the following statement changes when the underlined words are removed.

Countless people are seriously maimed in traffic accidents. → People are hurt in traffic accidents.

Read the excerpts. Evaluate them with a partner and answer the questions.

1

UBI supporters say that the policy could be a massive improvement to economic efficiency. Implementing UBI could save societies money by replacing other, more complicated welfare programs. The taxes currently used to fund those programs and their administration could be lowered. Furthermore, under a UBI, people enduring dull, miserable jobs would be free to find work or start businesses they actually like.

DETECTING LANGUAGE Underline any words or phrases that appeal to the reader's emotions.

PURPOSE Why does the author use this kind of language?

____

2

As a nation grows increasingly prosperous, it seems clear that it should also change its policies to better protect life, liberty, and the pursuit of happiness. By ensuring basic human needs with a UBI, a government can not only help millions but also create the necessary conditions for continued growth and productivity.

DETECTING LANGUAGE Underline any words or phrases that appeal to the reader's emotions.

PURPOSE Why does the author use this kind of language?

____

IDEAS IN DISCUSSION

1. What does your country do to provide citizens with basic human needs?

2. What can governments do to reduce joblessness?

3. What are the possible disadvantages of a UBI program?

4. Do you think poverty and crime are connected?

5. Do you agree with the regulation in Gyeonggi province that limits UBI spending to registered local businesses? Do you think this rule is fair? Why or why not?

IDEAS IN WRITING

1. Write a paragraph about what your country's government does to ensure your basic needs.

2. Analyze the potential benefits and drawbacks of implementing a universal basic income (UBI).

3. State whether you support universal basic income (UBI) providing reasons for your stance.

4. Write about how new technologies and automation have influenced the job market. Do they create more opportunities or contribute to job losses and economic inequality?

5. If automation and new technologies make the economic gap between different groups wider, what should a government do to help close that gap?

SOCIOLOGY

UNIT 9-2 How Do We Choose Our Friends?

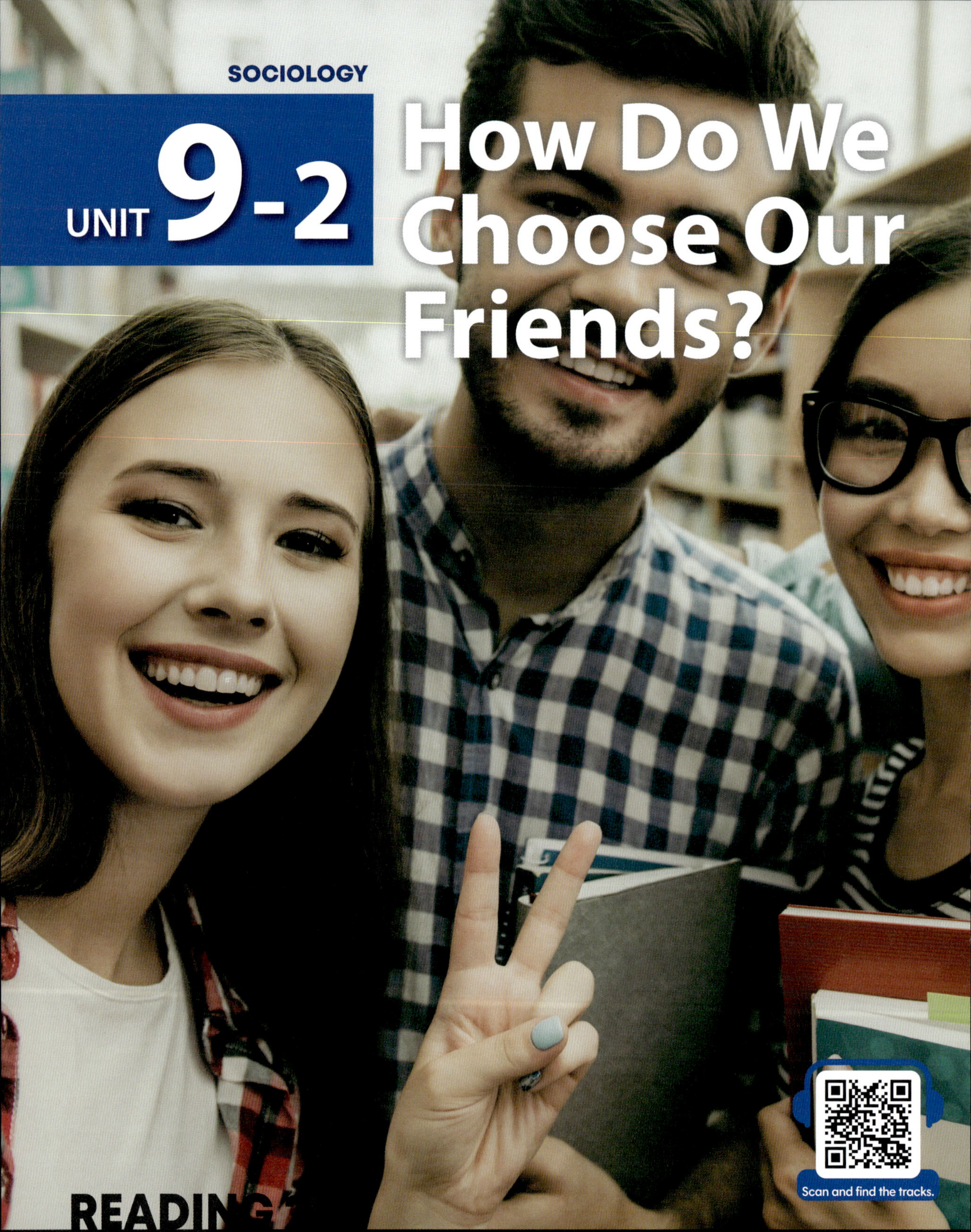

Scan and find the tracks.

READING 1

SKILLS

Reading Skill:
Summarizing

Critical-Thinking Skill:
Understanding Key Terms

WARM-UP QUESTIONS

1. How did you meet your closest friend?

2. Have you ever ended a friendship because of something you or your friend did?

3. How many contact numbers do you have stored on your cell phone? Among them, how many people would you consider your "close friends"?

4. What is the most important trait you look for when making friends?

5. What do your close friends have in common?

BEFORE YOU READ

Rank the statements from 1 (most agree with) to 6 (least agree with). Discuss your rankings with a partner.

__________ A friend should always be honest with me.

__________ A friend should have a background similar to mine.

__________ A friend should share my interests.

__________ A friend will always help me when I'm in need.

__________ A friend will always keep my secrets.

__________ A friend will share all he or she has with me.

VOCABULARY PREVIEW

1 Read the sentences. Circle the words closest in meaning to the words in bold.

1. People **seek** friends who have excellent qualities.
   a. suggest b. trust c. look for

2. The way people choose friends is more **complex** than many might think.
   a. complicated b. serious c. surprising

3. It's **obvious** that people tend to be friends with the people nearest them.
   a. silly b. clear c. common

4. People are more **inclined** to talk with people who are closer to them.
   a. willing b. expected c. required

5. **Residents** of the same floor are more likely to become friends.
   a. inhabitants b. communities c. locals

6. The students were given seats **randomly** in the classroom.
   a. strictly b. in pairs c. by chance

7. Rhesus macaques are friendlier with monkeys that have a higher social **status**.
   a. position b. ability c. group

8. The **hypothesis** states that people are friendlier with people they see as socially significant.
   a. argument b. theory c. topic

2 Match the words in section 1 above to their definitions below.

________ : difficult to understand or find an answer to because of having many different parts

________ : an idea or explanation for something that is based on known facts but has not yet been proved

________ : likely or wanting to do something

________ : easy to see, recognize, or understand

________ : in a way that happens, is done, or is chosen by chance rather than according to a plan

________ : a person who lives or has their home in a place

________ : to try to find or get something, especially something that is not a physical object

________ : an accepted or official position or rank, especially in a social group

HOW DO WE CHOOSE OUR FRIENDS?

Track 18

1. **Reading Skill: Summarizing**
   A summary restates the main points of a passage or work. Summarizing can help you focus and remember the most important information.

2. **Critical-Thinking Skill: Understanding Key Terms**
   Terms can have more than one possible meaning in context. Thus, it's important to identify key terms and understand the writer's definitions of the terms.

A study at Cornell University found that the average adult has 2.03 close friends. Yet researchers have also found that the same adult is likely to have about 150 social contacts, people they know and interact with regularly. This figure (now known as Dunbar's number) was named after the scientist Robin Dunbar and has been confirmed in other studies. But how is it that people have so many social contacts but only 2.03 close friends? How do we select the people who go from an **acquaintance**[1] to a friend? The common-sense answer is that we seek friendship in certain people because of their excellent personal qualities, but the answer coming from psychological research is more complex. Researchers have found that our choice of friends is largely affected by a combination of **proximity**[2], similarity, and self-interest.

To begin with the obvious, we're inclined to become friends with people who are nearby. We tend to form friendships with people we see in our neighborhood, school, or work. One famous US study from 1950 looked at residents of a two-story apartment building and found that people who lived on the same floor developed closer friendships than those who lived on different floors. In a 2008 experiment at a German university, students were randomly given seats for a single gathering. One year later, students who had sat near each other were more likely to be friends than those who had not.

[1] **acquaintance** *n.* someone who you know but do not know well
[2] **proximity** *n.* nearness

Of course, we do not develop relationships with everyone around us, so proximity isn't enough. Similarity is important as well. Psychologists use the term *homophily* to describe our preference for those with whom we have things in common, such as age, sex, race, class, physical characteristics, and interests. Research has found that the more of these characteristics people share, the more likely they are to become friends. Brain images show that we find it easier to **empathize**[3] with those we view as similar to ourselves. One theory is that homophily developed as a side effect of our natural preference for those who share our DNA—our relatives.

Self-interest is also a key factor in how we form friendships. Evolutionary psychologists reason that the behavior of our closest relatives—other primates—is much like our own. Thus, they look to non-human primates for clues to explain human friendship. Other primates also form warm, long-lasting relationships with individuals to whom they are not related. Primate friendship has perhaps been most thoroughly studied in the rhesus macaque. Rhesus macaques usually live in groups of about thirty. They do two things a lot: **cultivate**[4] friendships by **grooming**[5] each other and fight over food and mates. They especially tend to groom other monkeys of a higher social status, who are more likely to be helpful in a fight. In a study titled "The Alliance Hypothesis for Human Friendship," two psychologists present evidence that suggests human relationships are formed in a similar way to those among rhesus monkeys. The authors looked at how people ranked their friends on a social networking site. While social status didn't matter, people tended to highly rank the friends who, in turn, ranked them highly. Researchers believe that this is because, like the macaque, we sometimes need **allies**[6]. And the more a friend cares, the more likely they are to help us in a conflict.

Of course, this is a pretty cold and incomplete view of friendship. Research helps explain how and why we make friends, but not how we sustain those friendships. Meeting by accident, having a few things in common, and having someone who will back you up in a fight isn't enough to make a friendship last for a lifetime. Also, even if the reasons appear less than **noble**[7], our feelings toward our friends can still be quite **genuine**[8]. The ways they make our lives better remain real. Consider one last finding from friendship research: having even one close friend can make you much happier than having none. And if you have 2.03, that's even better.

3	**empathize**	*v.*	to understand and share another's feelings
4	**cultivate**	*v.*	to try and make (something) grow
5	**groom**	*v.*	to clean and maintain
6	**ally**	*n.*	a person or group that agrees to defend another person or group
7	**noble**	*adj.*	having good moral qualities and behavior
8	**genuine**	*adj.*	real; true

COMPREHENSION CHECK-UPS

1. According to paragraph 1, what is Dunbar's number?

   a. The number of friends who live nearby
   b. The number of social-media contacts that people have
   c. The number of friends that people make in a lifetime
   d. The number of friends and acquaintances that people have

2. According to paragraph 2, which is NOT true about the German researchers?

   a. They began by seating students together at random.
   b. They asked about the students' friendships a year later.
   c. They confirmed that proximity is important in friendship.
   d. They concluded that students prefer sitting with people they know.

3. Read paragraph 2 and write the definition of *homophily*.

   ____

   ____

4. What can be inferred from paragraph 2?

   a. Luck plays a role in whom we become friends with.
   b. Neighbors are more likely to become friends than co-workers are.
   c. Many friendships formed during college do not last long.
   d. We tend to like people more if we don't see them too often.

5. According to paragraph 3, what is stated about homophily?

   a. It increases as proximity increases.
   b. There is evidence for it in brain activity.
   c. It may prevent people from showing empathy.
   d. Scientists believe that it runs in families.

6. According to paragraph 4, why do both macaques and humans cultivate friends?

a. To prevent future violent conflict
b. To improve their social positions
c. To get help against their enemies
d. To demonstrate how much they care

7. Which statement best restates the sentence, "While social status didn't matter, people tended to highly rank the friends who, in turn, ranked them highly." from paragraph 4?

a. People value others who value them.
b. Social status doesn't affect friendship.
c. Friendships are more important than social status.
d. People rank friends higher if they have high social status.

8. According to paragraph 5, the author states all of the following about friendships EXCEPT ________.

a. that our understanding of them is not complete
b. that we usually form them for morally good reasons
c. that research fails to show how we maintain them
d. that having just one improves your life significantly

9. In paragraph 5, why does the author say, "this is a pretty cold and incomplete view of friendship"?

a. To explain that the research lacks emotional understanding
b. To imply that much more research needs to be done
c. To claim that the studies are based on questionable data
d. To argue that friendship cannot be studied scientifically

10. Read paragraph 5. In what ways does the author consider the ideas about friendship incomplete?

____

____

MAPPING IDEAS

Read the statements that summarize the passage. Then put the answers in the correct order to complete the graphic organizer.

HOW DO WE CHOOSE OUR FRIENDS?				
PARAGRAPH 1	**PARAGRAPH 2**	**PARAGRAPH 3**	**PARAGRAPH 4**	**PARAGRAPH 5**
1. ________	**2.** ________	**3.** ________	**4.** ________	**5.** ________

STATEMENTS
a. However, this cold view of friendship lacks an understanding of how friendship is maintained.
b. In addition, we more easily build friendships with people who are like us.
c. Researchers also believe that we look for friends who will help us in a conflict.
d. Most of us have a small number of friends, and our reasons for choosing them are surprising.
e. Studies have found that we're more likely to become friends with someone in our immediate area.

VOCABULARY REVIEW

Fill in the blanks with the correct words from the box. Change the form if needed.

inclined	**randomly**	**empathize**	**hypothesis**
genuine	**complex**	**obvious**	**resident**

1. When the fire alarm went off, the apartment building ______________ quickly began moving to the exits.
2. Salespeople are trained to smile and be helpful, but their friendliness isn't really ______________.
3. If you have to explain a(n) ______________ subject, try to use simple language and clear examples.
4. Charles Darwin developed the ______________ that species evolve through random changes in genes.
5. Jackie's extremely upset about losing her phone, and I can ______________ because I lost mine a year ago.
6. One ______________ solution to your financial problems is to find a better-paying job.
7. Few people are ______________ to eat outdoors in such chilly, wet weather.
8. Each student was ______________ given a topic to discuss for the next class.

CRITICAL-THINKING SKILL

Understanding Key Terms

Key terms in a passage might have more than one possible meaning that can only be determined from the context. Identifying key terms and understanding their definitions is important when analyzing a reading. This will prevent the reader from being misled or confused.

1 Find the author's definitions in the reading and complete the chart.

Key Term	Author's Definition
proximity	things which are nearby, in our 1. ______________, school, or work
similarity	things we have in common such as age, sex, race, class, physical traits, and 2. ______________
self-interest	the more likely a person is to defend us in a(n) 3. ______________
relatives	those who share our 4. ______________

2 Read the excerpt. Then check (✓) the sentence that uses the underlined word in the same way.

> One famous US study from 1950 looked at residents of a two-story apartment building and found that people who lived on the same floor developed <u>closer</u> friendships than those who lived on different floors.

_______ a. To hear the professor better, I had to move closer to the front of the room.

_______ b. My best friend moved into the same apartment as mine so we could be closer.

_______ c. I'm getting closer with my lab partner, so I'm sure she'll let me borrow today's notes.

_______ d. I think the idea that we befriend people who can benefit us is closer to the truth than we like to admit.

IDEAS IN DISCUSSION

1. Why do you think people need friends?

2. What do you like most about your closest friends?

3. Do you think the information in the reading applies to your friendships? Why or why not?

4. Among the three factors—proximity, similarity, and self-interest—which factor do you think contributes the most to forming friendships and why?

5. In an age where social media and online communication are prevalent, how significant is proximity in making friends? Do you think physical closeness is still as important as it used to be?

IDEAS IN WRITING

1. Write a paragraph about the conditions necessary for a real, long-lasting friendship.

2. Discuss the pros and cons of having many acquaintances and a few close friends. How can you achieve a balance between them for personal well-being?

3. Analyze the "Alliance Hypothesis for Human Friendship," which suggests that humans tend to value friends who help them during challenges. Discuss whether this hypothesis applies universally or if there are notable exceptions.

4. Write about your best friend and describe why he/she holds that special place in your life. Include your personal definition of what it means to be a 'best friend' and how your relationship reflects that definition.

5. Reflect on yourself: Do you believe you deserve to be considered a good friend to others? Why or why not? Provide three reasons to support your answer.

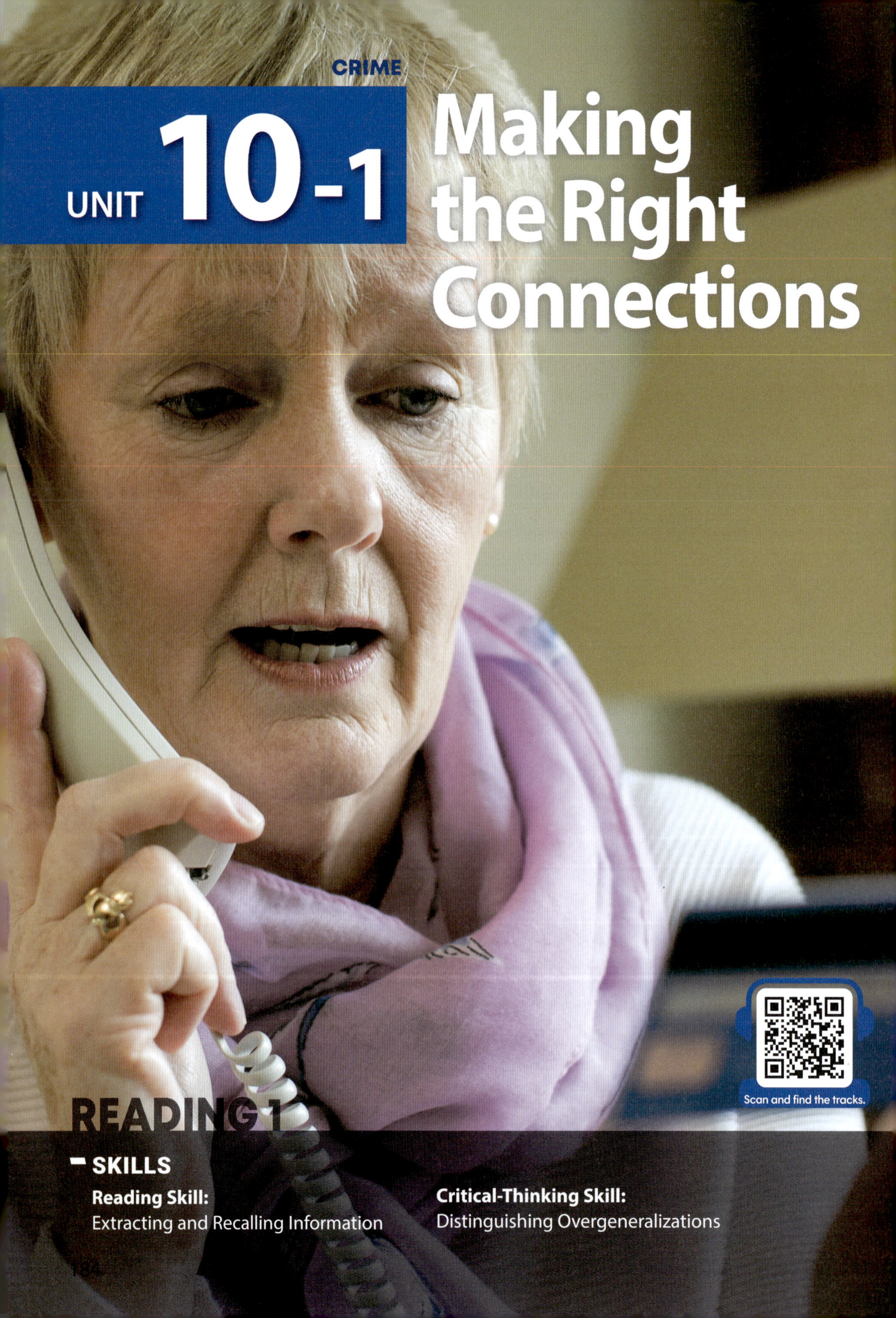

CRIME

UNIT 10-1 Making the Right Connections

Scan and find the tracks.

READING 1

SKILLS

Reading Skill:
Extracting and Recalling Information

Critical-Thinking Skill:
Distinguishing Overgeneralizations

WARM-UP QUESTIONS

1. Do you chat with people online that you have not met in real life?

2. Do you ever worry about your safety while you are online? How so?

3. Do you know what a digital footprint is and how it can affect your future?

4. Do you check a website's URL to ensure it's secure before entering personal information?

5. Do you regularly update your devices and apps to protect against security vulnerabilities?

BEFORE YOU READ

Rank the statements from 1 (most agree with) to 6 (least agree with). Discuss your rankings with a partner.

__________ I tend to trust the people I meet until I have a good reason not to.

__________ I am willing to help someone I trust who is in financial trouble.

__________ I have been tricked and hurt by someone I trusted before.

__________ I enjoy meeting and chatting with strangers on social media.

__________ I think it's easier to get close to people on the internet than in person.

__________ I believe you can make close friends online without ever meeting in person.

VOCABULARY PREVIEW

1 Read the sentences. Circle the words closest in meaning to the words in bold.

1. Some email scams promise to give money to a **respondent**.
   a. replier b. sender c. receiver

2. Many people are now aware of criminals' **schemes**, so new ones are being invented.
   a. swerves b. plots c. escapes

3. Bogus dating accounts often look very **convincing**.
   a. realistic b. significant c. aggressive

4. **Incidences** of dating site fraud increased during COVID-19 because people were at home and felt lonely.
   a. versions b. anecdotes c. occurrences

5. One US woman began **corresponding** with someone claiming to be a successful businessperson.
   a. comporting b. communicating c. coinciding

6. Even those who **initiated** contact should not assume the other user is genuine.
   a. established b. enlisted c. endured

7. Online scammers will often **induce** users to use text messaging, as it is more private.
   a. persuade b. expect c. allow

8. People running online scams will do **virtually** anything to avoid meeting face-to-face.
   a. barely b. instinctively c. practically

2 Match the words in section 1 above to their definitions below.

________ : having power to convince of the truth, rightness, or reality of something; plausible

________ : to communicate with a person by exchange of letters, emails, or texts

________ : an event

________ : to cause someone or something to do something

________ : to cause the beginning of something; to start or begin something

________ : someone who responds to a question or offer

________ : a plan or program of action, especially a crafty or secret one

________ : almost

MAKING THE RIGHT CONNECTIONS

Track 19

1. **Reading Skill: Extracting and Recalling Information**
   Readers can recall important information by skimming the text. Search for keywords, phrases, dates, or numbers to find information quickly.

2. **Critical-Thinking Skill: Distinguishing Overgeneralizations**
   An overgeneralization can be misleading and unfair. To avoid this, writers often use qualifying expressions such as *most, some, a few,* etc.

In the 1973 film *The Sting*, Robert Redford and Paul Newman play two **suave**[1] **con artists**[2]. The characters are sympathetic, and the film is a stylish, entertaining, and intelligent examination of human psychology. However, the reality of con tricks and those who perpetrate them is rarely as glamorous or **cerebral**[3]. Today, most scams take place **anonymously**[4] online as phishing, in which **unsolicited**[5] and often badly written emails appeal to people's sense of charity. A variation called spear-phishing asks for victims' account numbers, often promising a financial reward for the respondent.

But since many internet users now know the warning signs of these familiar schemes, personal online fraud increasingly relies on the victim unknowingly chatting with a criminal. For instance, "romance scams" use dating or social media sites to play on the human need for friendship, companionship, or love. Fake accounts can appear highly convincing, as fraudsters are willing to put in time and effort to appear entirely genuine. Once a scammer gains another user's trust—possibly over months or even years—requests begin for financial help with invented problems; these often include illnesses, travel expenses, or the cost of education.

It is estimated that one in ten profiles on dating sites is fake, and incidences of fraud increased during the COVID-19 pandemic as locked-down users looked online to combat loneliness. Back in

1	**suave**	*adj.*	very polite, pleasant, and usually attractive, often in a way that is false
2	**con artist**	*n.*	a person who deceives others to make them give money away
3	**cerebral**	*adj.*	demanding or involving careful thinking and mental effort
4	**anonymously**	*adv.*	without the name of someone being known or made public
5	**unsolicited**	*adj.*	not asked for

2015, US dating site users reported being tricked out of $33 million, but in 2020, this number jumped to $201 million. In Hong Kong alone, around 700 people reported being **defrauded**[6] via dating sites between January and September 2020—a fifty-percent increase on the previous year. Hong Kong police confirmed that almost ninety percent of victims were female and that together they had lost around HK$160.8 million (approximately $30 million). Older victims, who tend to be wealthier, are also fairly common, though victims in Hong Kong ranged from fifteen to eighty-five.

After initial contact on social media, a sixty-seven-year-old Chicago woman named Ellen Floren began corresponding with a charming man called "James Gibson," who claimed to be an executive. Conveniently, whenever Ms. Floren arranged to meet Mr. Gibson for coffee or lunch, there was always a last-minute problem: a sudden business trip or emergency. Before long, Mr. Gibson asked Ms. Floren for $100 as he'd run out of Netflix credit while on a flight. She agreed but became suspicious when he soon announced he'd also left some tools in a taxi and needed $2,600 to replace them. Wisely, Ms. Floren refused and contacted the police. Stories like hers can provide useful lessons to guide us in building friendships online.

1. When using social media, don't accept friend requests from strangers. But equally, don't feel a false sense of security because you were the one who initiated contact; scammers will often post hundreds of fake accounts and wait for other users to contact them.
2. A photo or specific information about ages, jobs, or locations is no guarantee that an account is genuine. Scammers may use real names and matching photographs so that when searched for online, they appear convincing. Similarly, they will often claim that their webcams are broken in order to avoid identification.
3. Most scammers will quickly want to move away from social media and induce you to use a more secure and private means of communication, such as texts or phone calls. Until you are sure, stick to the hopefully **reputable**[7] platform on which you met them.
4. Never send money, gift cards, or bank details to someone you have only met online. Scammers will do or say virtually anything to avoid meeting and will often claim to be on the other side of the world. In fact, it is common for them to request money for a flight so that they and their victim can finally "meet in person."

Although cybercrime cost the world economy an estimated $1 trillion in 2020, it is important to remember that not everyone is out to defraud you. In fact, communicating online is an increasingly common way to meet people with shared interests or even find the love of your life. But when online, ask questions and get to know someone slowly—just as you would in the real world. And remember, when attempting to build a friendship or relationship, the last thing an honest person would do is ask for money.

[6] **defraud** *v.* to take someone's money or goods illegally by deception
[7] **reputable** *adj.* held in high esteem; thought of favorably

COMPREHENSION CHECK-UPS

1. According to paragraph 1, all of the following are true EXCEPT ________.

a. a 1970s film made con tricks seem interesting and exciting
b. in the real world, con tricks are less glamorous than on screen
c. often, the emails sent in online scams are not well constructed
d. spear-phishing usually relies on people's sympathy for others

2. According to paragraph 2, how has internet scammers' behavior changed?

a. They now attempt to meet people in person and take their money.
b. They invest larger amounts of money to make themselves seem legitimate.
c. They are willing to spend more time making internet users trust them.
d. They have developed complicated programs to hide their identities.

3. Read paragraph 2. Write the two-word phrase that describes con tricks on dating sites.

____

4. In paragraph 2, why does the author use the phrase "play on the human need"?

a. To show how scammers enjoy the things that they do
b. To say that con artists understand and use psychology
c. To suggest that scammers are good actors
d. To imply that online fraud is based on greed

5. What can be inferred from paragraph 2?

a. Phishing and spear-phishing are less successful than they previously were.
b. Most social-media sites are taking a lot of measures to fight fraud.
c. Con artists tend to be highly educated and sophisticated.
d. Many scammers do have genuine financial difficulties.

6. **Which of the following is NOT stated in paragraph 3?**

a. In 2015, US dating site users were tricked out of more than $30 million.
b. In Hong Kong during COVID-19, cases of fraud on dating sites doubled.
c. In 2020, the majority of fraud victims in Hong Kong were women.
d. Hong Kong police found that collectively, victims had lost $30 million.

7. **Read paragraph 3. Write any qualifying expressions that might signal a generalization.**

____

____

8. **According to paragraph 4, why was Mr. Gibson unable to meet Ms. Floren?**

a. He lived thousands of miles away from Chicago.
b. After losing his tools, he could not afford the cost of a flight.
c. His business was about to relocate to another city.
d. His plans were affected by unexpected events.

9. **Which statement best restates the sentence, "Most scammers will quickly want to move away from social media and induce you to use a more secure and private means of communication, such as texts or phone calls." from paragraph 7?**

a. Con artists want to communicate off social media in more private settings.
b. Scammers often use social media to get access to private information.
c. Con artists prefer to use webcams and social media to contact victims.
d. Scammers prefer talking on the phone because they can be more persuasive.

10. **According to the four tips, how can a scammer give someone a false sense of security?**

a. By chatting with a person through their webcam
b. By not approaching other users first
c. By giving a user many compliments
d. By offering to send money or other gifts

MAPPING IDEAS

Read the opening sentences from the reading and match them to the correct detail sentences below.

MAKING THE RIGHT CONNECTIONS		
PARAGRAPH #	**OPENING SENTENCES**	**DETAILS**
Paragraph 1	In the 1973 film *The Sting*, Robert Redford and Paul Newman play two suave con artists.	**1.** ______
Paragraph 2	But since many internet users now know the warning signs of these familiar schemes, . . .	**2.** ______
Paragraph 3	It is estimated that one in ten profiles on dating sites is fake, . . .	**3.** ______
Paragraph 4	After initial contact on social media, a sixty-seven-year-old Chicago woman named Ellen Floren began corresponding with a charming man called "James Gibson," who claimed to be an executive.	**4.** ______
Paragraph 6	A photo or specific information about ages, jobs, or locations is no guarantee that an account is genuine.	**5.** ______
Paragraph 9	Although cybercrime cost the world economy an estimated $1 trillion in 2020, . . .	**6.** ______

DETAILS

a. Before long, Gibson asked Ms. Floren for $100 as he'd run out of Netflix credit while on a flight.
b. Scammers may use real names and matching photographs online so that they appear convincing.
c. When a scammer gains another user's trust, they request financial help with invented problems that often include illness, travel expenses, or the cost of education.
d. In Hong Kong, around 700 people reported being defrauded via dating sites . . .
e. Today, most scams take place anonymously online as phishing.
f. When trying to build a friendship or relationship, an honest person would never ask for money.

VOCABULARY REVIEW

Fill in the blanks with the correct words from the box. Change the form if needed.

respondent	**scheme**	**convincing**	**incidence**
correspond	**initiate**	**anonymously**	**unsolicited**

1. Mandy has been ______________ with her high school friends who live abroad.

2. ______________ to the survey said that they preferred the original taste of the yogurt.

3. The film was spoiled because the actor's Scottish accent was not ______________.

4. The man who ______________ the fight was taken away by the police.

5. The thief's ______________ involved stealing people's tax returns.

6. The man got several ______________ phone calls from telephone marketers.

7. Tony made a donation to the charity ______________ because he didn't want any attention.

8. This week, there have been several ______________ of car theft, which authorities are investigating.

CRITICAL-THINKING SKILL

Distinguishing Overgeneralizations

An overgeneralization is an overly broad statement that can be misleading and unfair. To avoid this, writers often use qualifying expressions. These include *most, some, a few, several, usually, often, probably, likely, and may/might,* among others.

Read the excerpts. Evaluate them with a partner and answer the questions.

1 Today, most scams take place anonymously online as phishing, in which unsolicited and ________ badly written emails appeal to people's sense of charity. A variation called spear-phishing asks for victims' account numbers, ________ promising a financial reward for the respondent.

QUALIFYING EXPRESSION Choose the word that CANNOT be used in both blanks to best complete the excerpt.

a. probably b. rather c. often d. usually

SUMMARIZE Write a short summary of the excerpt.

____

2 Once a scammer gains another user's trust—________ over months or even years—requests begin for financial help with invented problems; these ________ include illnesses, travel expenses, or the cost of education.

QUALIFYING EXPRESSION Choose the word that can be used in both blanks to best complete the excerpt.

a. may b. might c. most d. probably

SUMMARIZE Write a short summary of the excerpt.

____

IDEAS IN DISCUSSION

1. Why do you think meeting people online is so popular today?

2. How can we find out if the people we meet online are genuine?

3. How could social-media companies make meeting people online safer?

4. How do scammers trick people into falling for their scams? What are the signs to look out for?

5. Why do you think people who fall for romance scams might be embarrassed to talk about it? How can we make it easier for them to speak up?

IDEAS IN WRITING

1. Write a paragraph about the safety of meeting people online and include some advice of your own on how to stay safe.

2. Describe a time when you or someone you know was targeted by an online scammer. What were the red flags? How did you or they handle the situation?

3. Write a paragraph arguing for stricter regulations on social media platforms to combat online scams. What specific measures can be taken?

4. Write a guide for older adults on how to protect themselves from online scams. What are the key tips and tricks?

5. Imagine you are a police officer investigating a case of online fraud. What would your first steps be in tracking down a scammer?

CRIME

UNIT 10-2 Prime Targets

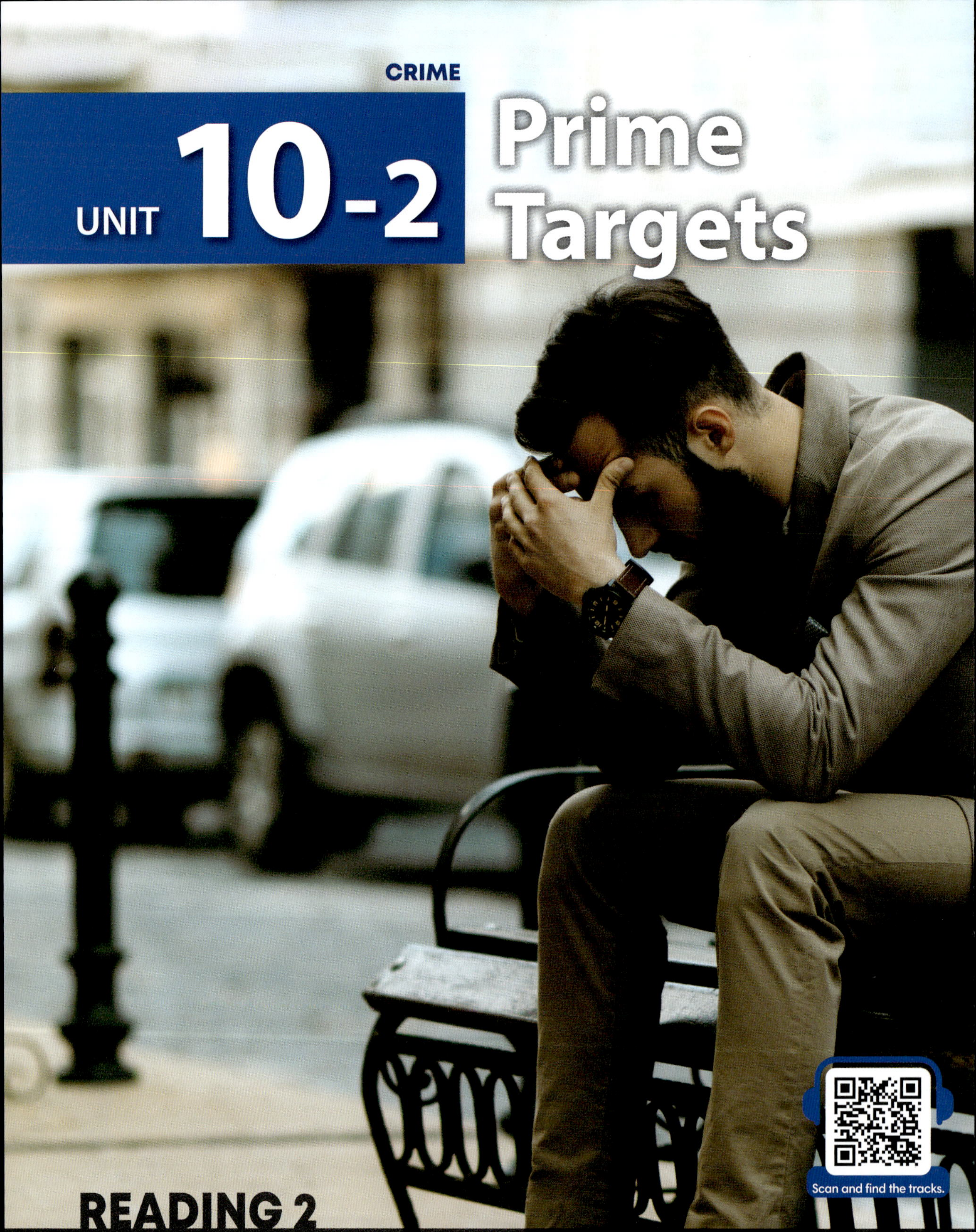

Scan and find the tracks.

READING 2

SKILLS

Reading Skill:
Extracting and Recalling Information

Critical-Thinking Skill:
Distinguishing Overgeneralizations

WARM-UP QUESTIONS

1. How can you tell if you can trust someone?
2. Have you or anyone you know been tricked by someone? What happened?
3. What are some common scams that target tourists? Have you heard any stories about people getting scammed while traveling?
4. What's a good way to stay safe when using public transportation in a foreign country?
5. When traveling to a new country, why is it a good idea to learn about local customs and etiquette?

BEFORE YOU READ

Read the statements. Check (✓) whether you agree or disagree with each statement. Discuss your answers with a partner.

	Strongly disagree	Disagree somewhat	Agree somewhat	Strongly agree
1. People who fall for fraud are usually unintelligent.				
2. I would never be a victim of fraud.				
3. I can tell if someone is trustworthy or not.				
4. People on vacation are more vulnerable to con artists.				
5. People who are unhappy or struggling with their finances are at greater risk from con artists.				

VOCABULARY PREVIEW

1 Read the sentences. Circle the words closest in meaning to the words in bold.

1. Visitors from other countries are **prime** targets for most scammers.
   a. valuable b. established c. choice

2. Tricksters often **exploit** non-locals who are unfamiliar with the local money.
   a. ensure b. abuse c. wield

3. Because tourists are not familiar with the local **currency**, they can be easily tricked.
   a. system b. money c. manners

4. Scammers know tourists won't **file** complaints since they cannot speak the local language.
   a. register b. classify c. resolve

5. It is relatively common for older people to be tricked into losing money or even their entire **estate**.
   a. sacrifices b. regimes c. fortune

6. Scam victims are likely to have struggled financially in the **period** leading up to the crime.
   a. outcome b. locus c. time

7. Con artists often befriend internet dating site users and later **extract** money from them.
   a. receive b. remove c. reduce

8. Scam victims often feel angry at themselves as they think they have **participated** in the crime.
   a. cooperated b. consulted c. compelled

2 Match the words in section 1 above to their definitions below.

________ : something, such as coins or banknotes, that is in circulation as a medium of exchange

________ : the assets, including money or property, owned by a person at the end of their life

________ : to make use of meanly or unfairly for one's own advantage

________ : to obtain; to take out

________ : to initiate something, such as a legal action, through proper formal procedure

________ : to take part, join in, or help

________ : a length of time during which a series of events or an action takes place

________ : the main or best

PRIME TARGETS

Track 20

1. **Reading Skill: Extracting and Recalling Information**
   Readers can recall important information by skimming the text. Search for keywords, phrases, dates, or numbers to find information quickly.

2. **Critical-Thinking Skill: Distinguishing Overgeneralizations**
   An overgeneralization can be misleading and unfair. To avoid this, writers often use qualifying expressions such as *most, some, a few, etc.*

Frequent travelers take pride in their ability to successfully **navigate**[1] unfamiliar places and cultures, which is why falling for a local **scam**[2] can feel so **humiliating**[3] for many tourists. Let's say, while exploring the Nanjing Road shopping district in Shanghai, you are stopped by two friendly young women who ask you to take a photo of them. You chat for a few minutes, and they mention that they're on their way to a tea ceremony and would like you to join them. Excited by the opportunity, you accept. Now imagine your shock when, after sipping tea for about half an hour, you notice that your **newfound**[4] friends are nowhere to be seen. In their absence, you are stuck with a bill for over $100. Sadly, this is not a misunderstanding—it is a common scam. While it's natural to feel foolish in this situation, victims can take **solace**[5] in the fact that they are not alone. **Cons**[6] happen every day and harm people all over the world, and the reason they work is the con artists' ability to identify easy targets.

As the situation demonstrated, foreign tourists are prime victims of scammers for several reasons. For one thing, if people can afford to travel abroad, their wallets are likely packed with plenty of cash and credit cards. Just as important, Chris Hagon, who heads a security consulting company, explains that "travelers are easy targets because they are unfamiliar with the

[1] **navigate** *v.* to find your way around or through
[2] **scam** *n.* a dishonest scheme; a fraud
[3] **humiliating** *adj.* extremely embarrassing
[4] **newfound** *adj.* recently discovered or established
[5] **solace** *n.* comfort or consolation when feeling sad or distressed
[6] **con** *n.* an instance of deceiving or tricking someone

environment, lack awareness, and are too trusting." Con artists tend to exploit something as simple as unfamiliarity with the local currency. For example, tourists have to check their change in Italy carefully: a two-euro coin looks similar to Italy's old 500-lira coin, but the 500-lira coin is worthless. Additionally, scammers know that tourists are reluctant to file complaints with the police because of time constraints and difficulty with the local language.

The elderly are also a common target for con artists and scammers. In the US alone, people sixty and older lose almost $3 billion a year to various frauds, many of which are **phony**[7] investment schemes—and often one where an entire estate is lost. Naturally, one might assume that this is due to a natural loss of mental sharpness as people age, but the true explanation isn't quite that straightforward. In a study performed at UCLA, researchers had adults of various ages look at photos of faces and evaluate how **trustworthy**[8] they seemed. Some of them showed classic signs of deception, such as an insincere smile. It turned out that younger adults were significantly better at identifying potential con artists than older adults were. MRI scans showed that younger people had greater activity in the anterior insula, a part of the brain that registers danger when looking at untrustworthy individuals.

So if people are young and in their home country, are they safe from con artists? Not necessarily. The third category of likely scam targets is one that everyone belongs to at least once in their lives: the emotionally distressed. A study of 11,000 US internet users compared the recent life experiences of those who had fallen for online scams and those who had not. It found that scam victims were more than twice as likely to have recently lost their jobs and were much more likely to have experienced a financial loss in the period before the incident. As one of the researchers put it, "Just as a weakened immune system lowers your resistance to disease, negative life events lower your resistance to fraud." Keenly aware of this, many con artists prey on the lonely and depressed through internet dating sites, where they befriend the victim and then extract money from them once they've gained their trust.

Victims of a scam may feel worse about their **predicament**[9] because they believe they actively participated in the crime. Thus the anger and stress over the financial loss are often mixed with embarrassment. If you're ever made a victim of a scam, remember that you're not the only one who's been fooled and that con artists are very good at what they do. They are clever **amateur**[10] psychologists who know when people are most vulnerable and how to take advantage of it. By arming yourself with knowledge, you can take the necessary steps to protect yourself from these predators.

7 **phony** *adj.* not genuine; not real
8 **trustworthy** *adj.* able to be relied on as honest or truthful
9 **predicament** *n.* an unpleasant situation that is difficult to get out of
10 **amateur** *adj.* engaging in something as a pastime rather than a profession

COMPREHENSION CHECK-UPS

1. According to paragraph 1, all of the following are true of the scam described EXCEPT ________.

a. local residents become friendly with a visitor
b. it takes place in a commercial part of the city
c. a business charges the tourist a large amount of money
d. the scammers pretend that they are unable to pay the bill

2. According to paragraph 2, all of the following are reasons that tourists are targeted EXCEPT ________.

a. they usually have a fair amount of money
b. they don't know the layout of the city well
c. they tend to visit the same areas of the city
d. they don't recognize the coins they are given

3. Read paragraph 2 and write any qualifying words or expressions that might signal a generalization.

____

____

4. What can be inferred from paragraph 2?

a. Tourists should trust locals who offer help.
b. Chris Hagon has been the victim of con artists.
c. Some scammers keep older coins to give to tourists.
d. Scammers target tourists who look unintelligent.

5. Which of the following is stated in paragraph 3?

a. Older people ordinarily trust younger people more.
b. People's awareness of risk usually declines with age.
c. Younger people are likely to trust older people more.
d. Dishonest people think more slowly than younger people.

6. Which statement best restates the sentence, "In the US alone, people sixty and older lose almost $3 billion a year to various frauds, many of which are phony investment schemes—and often one where an entire estate is lost." from paragraph 3.

   a. Elderly Americans lose billions yearly to investment fraud and other scams, and many lose everything.
   b. Con artists make $3 billion a year by defrauding Americans through investment schemes.
   c. Investment fraud is especially common in the US, where people lose $3 billion per year.
   d. Scammers target Americans aged sixty and over because they are most likely to have large estates.

7. Read paragraph 3. Which area of the brain controls how we recognize danger?

____

____

8. According to paragraph 4, what has an impact on one's probability of being a scam victim?

   a. Illness
   b. Economics
   c. Intelligence
   d. Location

9. In paragraph 4, why does the author use the phrase "a weakened immune system"?

   a. To compare being a scammer to an illness
   b. To contrast healthy people and scammers
   c. To illustrate that con artists lose eventually
   d. To explain why victims are vulnerable

10. According to paragraph 5, why should victims of scams not feel bad?

   a. Because scammers are experts and do their job well
   b. Because being trusting is a positive character trait
   c. Because there are ways to recover their losses
   d. Because they helped people who needed money

MAPPING IDEAS

Read the opening sentences from the reading and match them to the correct detail sentences below.

PRIME TARGETS		
PARAGRAPH #	**OPENING SENTENCES**	**DETAILS**
Paragraph 1	Frequent travelers take pride in their ability to successfully navigate unfamiliar places and cultures, which is why falling for a local scam can feel so humiliating for many tourists.	**1.** _______
Paragraph 2	As the situation demonstrated, foreign tourists are prime victims of scammers for several reasons.	**2.** _______
Paragraph 3	The elderly are also a common target for con artists and scammers.	**3.** _______
Paragraph 4	So if people are young and in their home country, are they safe from con artists?	**4.** _______
Paragraph 5	Victims of a scam may feel worse about their predicament because they believe they had actively participated in the crime.	**5.** _______

DETAILS

a. A study at UCLA found that people's ability to recognize risk and danger declines with age.
b. Con artists often trick tourists with simple scams such as manipulating the local currency.
c. People who are emotionally or financially distressed are also likely to be victims of a con.
d. Scams may make you feel foolish, but they happen every day to people all over the world.
e. Con artists are clever amateur psychologists who know exactly who to prey on.
f. Victims of a scam feel bad because they were outsmarted by the con artist.

VOCABULARY REVIEW

Fill in the blanks with the correct words from the box. Change the form if needed.

prime	**exploit**	**currency**	**period**
extract	**participate**	**navigate**	**solace**

1. On the weekend, Sarah and Steve will ______________ in a softball tournament.
2. The tourists could ______________ the city thanks to a special map application.
3. Although Spain now uses the euro, pesetas were once the local ______________.
4. After her husband's death, Jill found some ______________ in joining meetup groups.
5. In the ______________ between 1918 and 1933, Germany was known as the Weimar Republic.
6. The area surrounding Central Park is where the city's ______________ real estate is located.
7. It is unethical for politicians to ______________ their power for personal benefit.
8. Miners have the difficult job of ______________ materials from the earth.

CRITICAL-THINKING SKILL

Distinguishing Overgeneralizations

An overgeneralization is an overly broad statement that can be misleading and unfair. To avoid this, writers often use qualifying expressions. These include *most, some, a few, several, usually, often, probably, likely, and may/might*, among others.

Read the excerpts. Evaluate them with a partner and answer the questions.

1 Let's say, while exploring the Nanjing Road shopping district in Shanghai, you are stopped by two friendly young women who ask you to take a photo of them. You chat for a few minutes, and they mention that they're on their way to a tea ceremony and would like you to join them. Excited by the opportunity, you accept. Now imagine your shock when, after sipping tea for ________ half an hour, you notice that your newfound friends are nowhere to be seen. In their absence, you are stuck with a bill for ________ $100.

QUALIFYING EXPRESSION Choose the word that can be used in both blanks to best complete the excerpt.

a. about b. rather c. several d. often

SUMMARIZE Write a short summary of the excerpt.

____

2 The elderly are also a common target for con artists and scammers. In the US alone, people sixty and older lose almost $3 billion a year to various frauds, ________ of which are phony investment schemes—and often one where an entire estate is lost. Naturally, one might assume that this is due to a natural loss of mental sharpness as people age, but the true explanation isn't quite that straightforward. In a study performed at UCLA, researchers had adults of various ages look at photos of faces and evaluate how trustworthy they seemed. ________ of them showed classic signs of deception, such as an insincere smile.

QUALIFYING EXPRESSION Choose the word that CANNOT be used in both blanks to best complete the excerpt.

a. some b. many c. several d. quite

SUMMARIZE Write a short summary of the excerpt.

____

IDEAS IN DISCUSSION

1. What are some other scams people fall victim to?
2. Do you think there are a lot of con artists in your country? Why or why not?
3. What advice would you give to someone trying to avoid being scammed online?
4. Why do you think people are often more trusting of strangers when they are traveling? How can we balance being open to new experiences with being cautious?
5. What are the emotional and financial consequences of falling victim to a scam? How can victims recover from such experiences?

IDEAS IN WRITING

1. Write a paragraph about con artists and their ability to scam people out of their money.
2. Compare and contrast how younger and older people respond to scams and how they can protect themselves.
3. Research a specific type of scam, such as phishing or romance scams. Explain how these scams work and provide tips on how to avoid them.
4. Imagine you are planning to travel abroad for the first time. Write a paragraph explaining what steps you would take to avoid being scammed during your travels.
5. The article talks about how negative life events can lower a person's resistance to scams. Write a paragraph exploring how personal challenges, like losing a job or going through a difficult time, might make someone more susceptible to fraud.

MEMO